TEEN POWER
For Girls

—— 9 SECRETS TO ——
CONFIDENCE & SUCCESS

DEBORAH SAUNDERS

Teen Power for Girls: 9 Secrets to Confidence & Success

Deborah Saunders

First edition: 2021

Copyright © 2021: Deborah Saunders

All rights reserved

To discuss publishing your material
— self-publishing or regular publishing —
email: *submissions@AdirPress.com*
or visit us at *www.Adir Press.com*

No part of this publication may be translated, reproduced, stored in a retrieval system or transmitted in any form or by any means; electronic, mechanical, photocopying, recording or otherwise without prior permission from the copyright holder — except for a reviewer wishing to quote brief passages in connection with a review for inclusion in a magazine or newspaper.

TABLE OF CONTENTS

Introduction 5

Secret 1. Our Thinking Creates Our Feelings. 7

Secret 2. You Can Relax
About Your Moods and Emotions 18

Secret 3. You Are Always Valuable, No Matter What . 36

Secret 4. You Can Trust That Hashem
Is Pumping You with Awesome Resources. 46

Secret 5. You Always Have the Power to Choose . . . 62

Secret 6. No One Can Control You 78

Secret 7. Stress Comes from Your Mind,
Not from Life 97

Secret 8. Let Go of the Past
and Stop Worrying About the Future 104

Secret 9. You Can Deal with Life
One Moment at a Time. 113

Bringing It All Together 122

WATCH: Four Steps to Your Teen Power 122

Final Words. 125

Approbations 126

INTRODUCTION

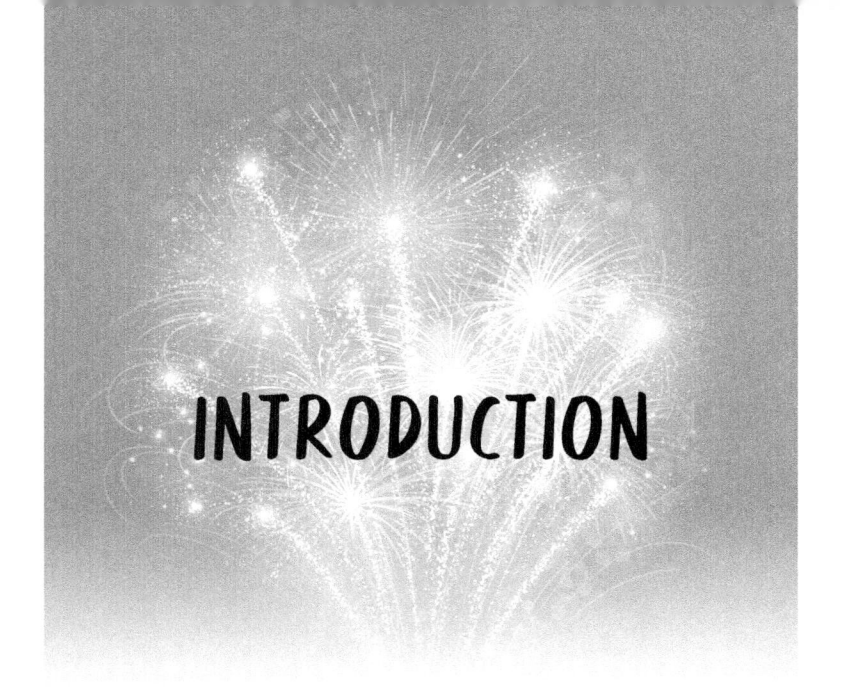

Dear Teen,

 I wrote this book as if you are sitting in front of me and we are chatting about life. I have probably never met you and possibly never will, but I can still have this conversation with you because you are a person, and as a person, you will experience themes — themes of challenges and themes of tools that are helpful when the going gets tough.

 Treat this book like a supermarket. Just like when we go shopping, we glance at the items we don't need and pick up the things that are useful to us, while reading this book you can take the ideas, examples, and suggestions that work for you and not worry about the rest. You may well find that some things written in this book will be helpful to you at certain times and other things at other times. Keep reading it so that you can get the full benefit.

 This book has been written with input, advice, and examples from many incredible teenagers (you know who you are . . .), and I am grateful to all of them for making this project possible. I am also grateful to Keren Keet for designing the cartoons which have greatly enhanced the book, Yaeli Harari for creating many graphics throughout the book and Rabbi Moishe Kormornick and his expert team at Adir Press for orchestrating the publishing process.

I would also like to thank my amazing husband Yehuda, for his invaluable input and support throughout this project.

I have put a lot of effort into writing this book. Now I hand it over to you. You will decide how to use it. You will decide if you let yourself be open-minded about finding new and improved ways of living life. No one can decide that but you!

Now let's get started . . .

SECRET 1

Our Thinking Creates Our Feelings

So, there's the first secret. You may be thinking, "What's the big deal? So what if our thinking creates our feelings? What difference does it make?" But the truth is, this secret can really change our lives. The fact that what we feel comes from our *thinking*, not from whatever is going on around us, means that it is not the comment someone just made, the exams you have coming up, or the situation that is going on in your family that creates your experience. It is the *thinking* that you have about the things that are going on around you that creates what you feel in each moment.

You see, we can look at a home, school, or social situation and think about it in a secure way, and we will feel secure about it. We can also take the same situation and get into an insecure frame of mind, and we will feel insecure about it.

Look at the following cartoon which explains how our thinking about different situations can totally change how we see them:

INSECURE THINKING   **SECURE THINKING**

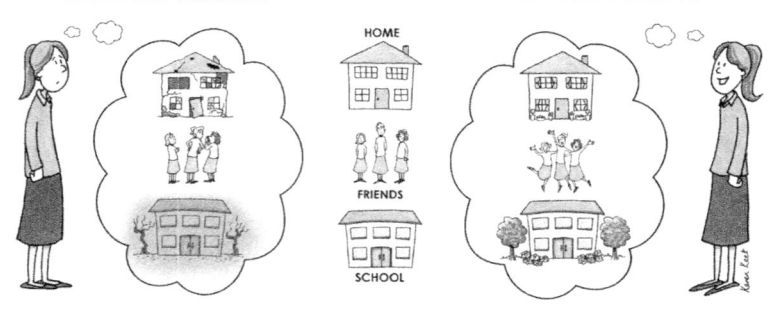

When we understand that what we feel does not come from *outside us*, it comes from *inside us*, we stop waiting for people or circumstances to change before we can feel better. We know that there is always another way to look at and experience anything that is going on outside of us. This knowledge of the inside-out experience of life can change the way we see ourselves, tackle challenges, enjoy friendships, and steer towrd success and away from failure. We start to realize how strong we are as people and find that we can choose to respond to anything in the best way possible.

Don't worry if this does not make all that much sense to you yet! It might take time for it to sink in, but it is well worth the wait. This book is full of examples and stories to help bring this important point home to you so that you can use it in a way that can change your life for the better.

Tammy's Secure and Insecure Thinking

Tammy was not enjoying school. Her classmates would constantly make comments about her being studious and make fun of how much the teachers liked her. Tammy would then get upset and either say hurtful things back or swallow her being studious and make fun of how much the teachers liked her. She would sometimes move into *insecure thinking* and begin to feel insecure, lonely, and like giving up in school. She thought that her uncomfortable feelings were coming from the girls, not realizing that in reality, they were coming from the insecure thinking she was having about the girls' behavior.

Tammy can realize that the girls are doing the wrong thing by making these comments, but she has the power to decide whether to react. She has the potential to have *secure thinking* about her situation. A fish swimming in water has no choice whether to take the bait at the end of a fishing rod or not. It is automatic. It sees it, it bites it, and it gets caught. Tammy is not a fish, she is a person! That means that she has the power to choose whether to "take the bait" and get into a fight or to deal with the situation in a better way.

Insecure thinking

Secure thinking

If Tammy realizes that her experience can only ever be from her mind in the moment, she can see that as her insecure thinking gets quieter, secure thinking will flow, and she will feel much calmer and more focused. It's not that Tammy is pretending that the girls' behavior isn't happening; she is just stopping to take it so personally. It doesn't threaten her. Tammy is honest about what is going on in school, but she finds a new way of dealing with it. She feels capable of tackling the situation, and if she needs help, she knows whom to get this help from and has the confidence to do it. This is Tammy in her secure thinking. This is Tammy listening to her inner voice.

We all have an "inner voice." I think of it like a GPS helping us navigate through life situations, relationships, and decisions. We can hear this voice more clearly when we are in secure thinking, and that is why we feel more confident. When insecure thinking comes in, we can find it hard to hear our inner voice, and we become confused and unsure of ourselves.

> If you knew that there was a more confident way of seeing anything that is bothering you how would you feel?

The Department Store

One of my favorite stores in England is House of Fraser, a department store with many floors. If you look out from the fifth-floor windows, you can see quite a distance. You can see roads, trees, people, perhaps some birds, and a view beyond. If you go down to the ground floor, however, although you are in the same building, all you can see is a small part of a road. Different parts of the same building can show totally different views, depending on where you are looking from.

We all have different "floors" inside us through which we can see any situation in life. When we are on the higher floors, we feel secure, focused, connected to others, and hopeful. When we are on the lower floors, we feel stuck, insecure, and sorry for ourselves.

We can look at *any* situation from the highest or lowest floor. It is the floor we are on that creates our feelings, not the outside circumstances.

Which Floor Are We On?

The drawing below shows clearly how "higher floors" of thinking and "lower floors" of thinking are so different.

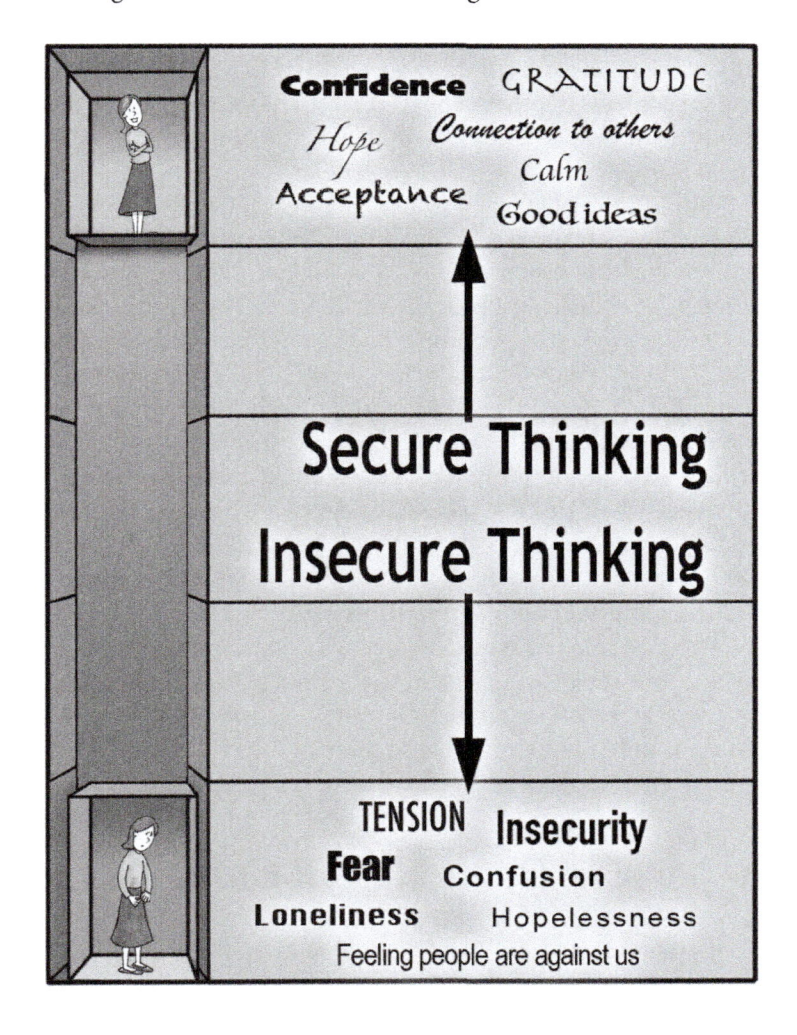

Confidence GRATITUDE
Hope Connection to others
Acceptance Calm
Good ideas

Secure Thinking

Insecure Thinking

TENSION Insecurity
Fear Confusion
Loneliness Hopelessness
Feeling people are against us

The good news is that there is an "elevator" which can easily transport us to a higher floor from one moment to the next. This explains how we can feel better about the same thing at a different time. We can shift to a different floor and look at the same situation with more confidence and in a more relaxed way. Hashem is the One who operates this elevator; He is the One Who can shift us out of our insecure thinking to secure thinking. But although Hashem controls the elevator, it is up to us to step inside and push the button. It is up to us to want to feel better and do what we can to help ourselves.

Ruti, a young teenager, was constantly dieting and worrying about her weight. She would sometimes get into a downward spiral of thinking about how scared she was of gaining weight and then feeling a lot of fear and lack of confidence. This is Ruti on the "basement" level of her building. She did not have a choice about going to the basement level; she just found herself there. She could accept that she was in the basement and trust that even in that moment of difficulty — even as she felt so low about herself and her life — there was a higher level ready and waiting for her to experience when Hashem would decide to move her up. She could choose to invest in her own happiness and do things that would help her feel better, like finding someone she trusted to speak to, until she returned to her secure thinking.

There is never a situation that locks us into a low floor. When we can experience secure thinking, time and again we will see that there is always an opportunity to move forward, learn from mistakes, and invest in good friendships.

The Hot and Cold Game

It's like the Hot and Cold game that kids like to play, where someone goes out of the room and then has to come back in and find a hidden object. As they get closer, everyone shouts, "Warm!" or "Hot!" or even "Boiling!" As they step further away, everyone shouts, "Cool!" or "Cold!" or even "Freezing!" Our feelings tell us whether we are nearer to or farther away from our inner voice. The more focused, clear, hopeful, and confident we feel (or any other themes of the "higher floor"), the closer we are to secure thinking and the more seriously we should take our thinking. The more tense, insecure, confused, and hopeless we feel, the less seriously we need to take our thinking.

The Welsh Vacation

One summer, I went with my family on a vacation to the Welsh countryside. We'd planned to have a barbecue when we arrived, but when we got there, it was pouring, so barbecued chicken soon changed to grilled cheese sandwiches! We huddled in our cottage and played board games, occasionally gazing out the window at the darkness outside, listening to the rain, and dashing to the car to get something.

The next morning, we woke up to sunlight streaming in through the windows. We went outside and could not believe how beautiful the grounds were. There was a huge lawn with lots of space for the children to play as well as countryside paths, a beautiful stream, and plenty of sheep. It struck me that we were in the same location as we had been the night before, when it had seemed so dark and confined, but now we realized how expansive it really was and the opportunity and potential we had before us. We went from being closed in and huddled to exploring and enjoying the expanse.

Noa was struggling in high school. She felt like a failure and that she was closed in and trapped in her situation. Although she is a creative girl with a great personality, she felt like she was so stuck. She had the potential of a great and productive life but couldn't see it because of the "rain" in her mind, which kept her huddled inside. In time, Noa was able to see the huge potential all around her, and even though it often still rained for Noa, she was able to feel hopeful about the future and remember the opportunities she knew were available to her. She stopped limiting herself by living according to the rainy weather — by making decisions or taking her thinking too seriously when she was experiencing a "closed-in" feeling. She began to wait for these dark moments to pass, ready to allow herself to enjoy the opportunities available to her.

All the different levels of clarity can potentially operate in any situation for each of us. The higher up we are, the more perspective we have, and the more able we are to connect to simple, profound truth. The lower the level of clarity, the more complicated life seems, and the more closed in we feel by it.

When one of my daughters was three years old, she was once throwing a tantrum as three-year-olds tend to do. She was very sad about everything, and I thought of an idea to cheer her up. I said, "Just think, soon it will be your birthday and you are going to be four." She looked at me for a second and then began to moan, "I don't want to be four, I want to be five!"

This is not just a cute story, it is the story of each of us when we are at a low level of clarity. We see lack in everything we look at. We see lack in ourselves, the past, the future, and those around us. We can breathe a sigh of relief when we realize that it is not our life that is lacking, it is our frame of mind — and that is very changeable!

What Other Teens Have Said About Secret 1

> When you recognise that you are in insecure thoughts, doesn't mean they necessarily go away but you can work on moving up.

> A situation isn't terrible. It's just what we think about it. We can decide how we think about it.

> Insecure thinking will pass. It's useful to remember that.

SECRET 2

You Can Relax About Your Moods and Emotions

Really? You can relax about your moods? How can you relax about them when you are still feeling them?

I get this question! I hope that this chapter will show you how life-changing it can be to stop fighting your moods and start to take them less seriously.

Am I the Only One?

First let's get one thing straight: You are in very good company if you get into bad moods or feel insecure sometimes. Everyone does! We may sometimes feel overwhelmed by the intensity of the ups and downs in our moods. We may feel threatened that they will overpower us, and the world can look like a dark place. This chapter aims to help you understand your moods and how to deal with them well.

The Hurricane Simulator

I like to think of moods like a simulator.

A few years ago, my husband and I took our kids to Blue Planet Aquarium in Chester, England. When we came to the hall where we could sit down and give the kids snacks, I noticed that at the back of the room there was something I had not seen before. It was a hurricane simulator, which is a booth that sends out a strong wind, making the people inside it feel like they are experiencing a hurricane. As I was sitting with my family and eating calmly, we watched a woman and her daughter inside the simulator clinging onto the rail in the booth, their hair flying in all directions. They were clearly having the best time!

It looked like this:

I realized that this is exactly how our feelings work. We are in a calm room of being okay with life, and then, without realizing it, we are headfirst in a simulator. Our mind starts pumping out thoughts, and we experience the feelings that mirror those thoughts.

When we have a thought, we automatically have a feeling alongside it which brings to life the energy of the thought as a sensory experience, so we feel it. When our mind is full of angry thoughts, we feel angry; when it is full of insecure thoughts, we feel insecure; and when it is full of anxious thoughts, we feel anxious.

The same way that this woman and her daughter were feeling like they were in a hurricane and were experiencing it as if it was really happening even though they were in a calm room, we can feel all types of moods and feelings even though we are secure and okay.

When the money in the hurricane simulator booth ran out, the wind stopped and the woman and her daughter stepped out into the calm room. This is how our moods and feelings work. Have you ever gotten really stressed-out about something and afterward laughed about it, or at least felt calmer about it? This is an example of when you were in a simulator (of stress) and then, at some point, the "money ran out," so your stressful thoughts stopped pumping and you were back to your calm self.

Let me ask you a question: What would happen if that woman and her daughter woke up in the simulator? They would wake up in this crazy, strong experience of being in a hurricane without knowing what was going on. They would probably panic. It would have been the same experience of fake wind, but they would have been very scared and might have thought that the whole world had gone crazy!

What are the differences between the two situations that would cause them to laugh in one case and to be scared in another?

- Knowledge of what was happening (that they were in a simulator)

- The knowledge that it would end
- The knowledge that even though it felt real, it was not a real hurricane

Chaya can be fine and relaxed, and then, without realizing it, she can suddenly get really irritated and in a bad mood. She doesn't plan it; it just happens. The intensity of her feelings used to scare her. Understanding the three points above has really helped her to relax about her moods. This is what happened:

Knowing What Is Happening

Realizing that her moods are just simulators stopped Chaya from feeling trapped in them. She understood that she has stepped into a simulator but she is not losing herself, even when the feelings are really strong. She is Chaya; nothing will change that. When the simulation ends, she will step back into *feeling* okay, but she *is* okay even while the simulator is going.

Knowing That It Will End

Chaya has stopped seeing herself as stuck in the simulator forever. Even when her feelings are strong, she knows and reminds herself that they will pass and she will feel okay again. She pictures the hall with the simulator in it, herself in the simulator, and then herself back in the calm room. She will come out. It will end.

Knowing That Even If It Feels Real, It Is Not

Perhaps the most important thing for Chaya was learning that although she can be honest about how she feels, just because she feels it doesn't mean it's reality. She realized that her mind can tell her inaccurate things sometimes and she used to believe everything it told her.

Our feelings don't ask questions like "Should you really be angry at this person?" or "Is this really too much for you to handle or are you working yourself up?" They come to life anyway, and they can feel so true to us.

Chaya began to understand that the world has not gone crazy even if her thoughts have for the moment. She began to picture herself standing by the baggage carousel in the airport. She hears the machine start and sees the suitcases come down the conveyor belt. She does not take off every suitcase. She lets the suitcases pass by until hers arrives.

In the same way, Chaya began to watch her simulator thoughts pass by without feeling the need to get involved with them or take them too seriously. Then, when she had "calm room" thoughts which came with a clear, confident feeling, she took those thoughts seriously and acted on them.

One day, Chaya woke up in a bad mood. She thought, *Today is going to be so boring. My teacher will probably be annoyed with the class. I bet nothing will go right!* Then she began to laugh as she realized what was happening. Some heavy suitcases had flowed onto the carousel. These were not her suitcases. These thoughts were not accurate. She knew that because they made her feel tense and hopeless. She could wave and smile as they went past. She did not need to take them off and carry them. What a relief!

As she realized this and let these thoughts pass without getting involved in them, she began to feel better. She thought, *Let's just see how it goes. I will do the best I can. How about picking up a hot chocolate on the way to school?* Those were her suitcases! They were worth keeping!

Even while we are swaying with an insecure emotion, we are still ourselves. We are still dignified, worthy people experiencing that emotion. We don't lose who we are whether we are inside or outside of the simulator.

If you knew that you can let insecure thinking pass by, how would you feel?

The Snow Globe

If you shake a snow globe, the little white bits will float around. What happens if you leave the snow globe on the table for a few minutes and then look at it again? You'll notice that everything settled back into place naturally.

This idea gives us a great tip for how to deal with moods and emotions. Sometimes our mind is "shaken up," and lots of thoughts float around. When we don't stress about our thinking and let it settle, our mind gradually clears and we feel better. Sometimes we even laugh at ourselves as we remember our previous intense reaction! At the time something felt so dramatic and threatening, but afterward, when our mind settled, we saw things more clearly.

Rikki gets extremely annoyed when her younger sister Shani goes into her room and messes with her things. Her mind is like a shaken snow globe, with angry thoughts flying all over it. If she reacts from that place, she can't see clearly, so she will probably end up overreacting and saying or doing something she regrets. Rikki knows that the same way that the snow globe will naturally settle, so will her mind. Instead of storming downstairs to her sister, she learned to do something she enjoys, like drawing or reading, until her mind settles, and then she decides what to do. She has never regretted it yet!

If we accept that we are struggling or feeling a certain way, the snow globe is still and the bits settle. Then we can find an effective way to deal with the situation or feeling. When we judge ourselves, telling ourselves that we are silly or weak for feeling a certain way, we keep shaking the globe and the feelings only get stronger, making our view of the situation less clear.

We can learn this from little kids. They accept their feelings and vulnerability so easily. They don't judge themselves for how they are feeling; it makes no difference to how they see themselves. They are always on their own side. They don't fight themselves!

I was once carpooling in our seven-seater van, which has three rows of seats. I was in a rush, and there were several eight-year-old boys in various parts of the car. I announced, "Wherever you are, strap yourself in!" It then dawned on me that that is acceptance. Acceptance is "strapping in" wherever we find ourselves. Acceptance is being okay with ourselves wherever we are, whether we feel secure or insecure, happy or sad, clear-minded or confused, angry or calm. Then we can "drive" forward in life.

Accepting moods and feelings does not mean that we act on them. It means that we always have permission to feel the way we do, and we always have a choice about how we act. (Lots more about that in chapter 5.)

Dassy had a lot of negative, angry, hurt feelings toward her father. He never paid attention to her except to criticize her. She was relieved to learn that she could let her thoughts about her father pump through her and she could allow herself to feel the resulting experience of anger and hurt, but she will still be able to choose which thoughts and feelings to act on and which ones to let pass.

If someone is watching a show, it could be sad, exciting, scary, or funny, and the audience can be crying or laughing, or their hearts may start to race with fear. But as soon as they realize, "Oh, it's only a show," even though they may still feel those same feelings, the intensity is not as consuming because they are aware that they are sitting, safe and sound, watching this show, and they will leave the auditorium once the show is over.

Dassy was able to see when her mood was playing an "anger" or "resentment" show. Understanding that it was a show helped her to not take it too seriously and act on it. From her place in the "audience" she could decide what to do.

When we understand that our moods and feelings come from our thinking and we do not need to feel threatened by them, we can relax about our moods and then find a good way forward.

> If you knew that it is okay to relax and accept whatever you feel, what would change for you?

Join the Club

When I was preparing to write this book, I gave out a questionnaire to many teenagers in order to gain information. One of the questions I asked was "What are three of your fears?" Not one teenager answered, "I don't have any."

Everyone has fears! The question is which attitude we have toward our fears and insecurities and how we choose to deal with them.

It is amazing what a difference it makes when we relax about being scared rather than being scared of being scared. We can't control the insecurity, but we can control our attitude toward it, as shown below:

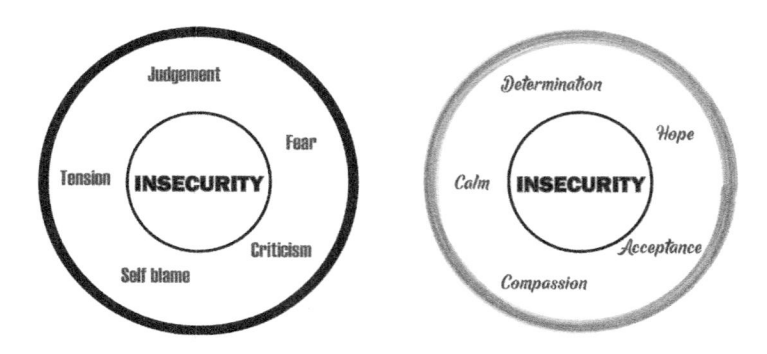

Left circle: Judgement, Fear, Tension, **INSECURITY**, Criticism, Self blame

Right circle: Determination, Hope, Calm, **INSECURITY**, Acceptance, Compassion

It's Okay

Shani used to dread going to places where there would be lots of people. When she'd arrive at an event, she would go into a "tension and insecurity simulator" and find herself tongue-tied and frustrated that she could not make conversation with people in the way she wanted to. She felt that she was making a fool of herself (although probably no one else saw it like that!) and that there must be something seriously wrong with her.

Why do I feel like this? I'm such a loser
I can't do this!
I don't know how to act!
What do I say?
Help!
I want to leave!
No one likes me!
Too many people!

It's ok to get tense and insecure sometimes
I can't do this!
I don't know how to act!
What do I say?
Help!
I want to leave!
No one likes me!
Too many people!
I'm still a valuable and worthy person
Karen Keet

Shani realized that her attitude toward her "insecurity simulator" was the key to feeling better. If she was okay with it instead of telling herself to be embarrassed about it, she would find herself relaxing and feeling more and more okay. The more relaxed Shani was about her social insecurity, the easier time she had while she was experiencing the simulator and the less often she found herself in it. Instead of getting lost in the simulator, she knew when she was in it, and although it was not always easy to feel that way, she relaxed about being in it. She stopped feeling so threatened by her fears and insecurities. She realized it is okay to get tense and insecure sometimes. She is still a valuable and worthy person, even while she is experiencing feelings. She would say to herself, "Do you know what? I am feeling really self-conscious right now, and I am finding it hard to speak." She couldn't believe how much it helped her to simply be okay with it.

Breathe!

When we are feeling nervous, without realizing it, our breathing can get quicker and shallower. Slowing down and deepening our breathing can really help. It is a practical move through which we can give ourselves the message that we can calm down. Here is a simple breathing technique: breathe in for a count of five, hold the breath for a count of five, and then breathe out for a count of five.

When Thoughts Disturb Us

Natalie would often have disturbing thoughts at night. It was like her scary thoughts would wait for her head to hit the pillow and then they would start to have a party! She definitely did not enjoy the party! She would feel very scared and unsettled, and as much as she tried to think about other things, it didn't work.

Then she would get annoyed with herself. She tried so desperately to control the thoughts and get them to stop, but everything she tried failed.

But then Natalie realized something which made a huge difference in her life. She realized that these thoughts *are not a part of her*. They would just jump into her mind. She didn't ask them to come and she could not force them out, but she could definitely choose to deal with them well.

It was such a relief for Natalie to understand that she cannot control her thoughts. The more she tried to push her thoughts out, the weaker she felt. Just like it wouldn't be fair for her to pressure herself to control the weather, it is not fair for her to expect herself to control her thoughts (because she can't).

Natalie realized that although these thoughts automatically brought with them an intense, insecure, panicky feeling, which was difficult to experience, the less she tried to force them out, the better she would feel. She could say to herself, "I am in my intense thinking now." She could then accept it, just like we can look out of the window, see that it's raining, and say, "Okay, that's disappointing" — we don't go out and try to fight the rain. Natalie can then trust that although she does not have control over this strong thinking, Hashem does, and she can hand this over to Him. She can also trust herself to have the resources to deal well with the things she *can* control.

In short, she cannot control her thinking, including when it comes, how strongly it comes, and how often it comes. She can, however, control her attitude toward it, how well she takes care of herself through it, and whether she is doing the best she can while it is around.

Natalie began to imagine herself as the driver of a car. Scary thoughts or uncomfortable feelings can jump into the passenger seat for a ride at any time of the day or night. She can keep driving and know that at some point the passenger will reach their destination and leave the car and she will remain in the driver's seat. Or she can feel threatened and controlled by the passenger, hand them the keys, and scuttle into the back seat! She can let her own thoughts bully her!

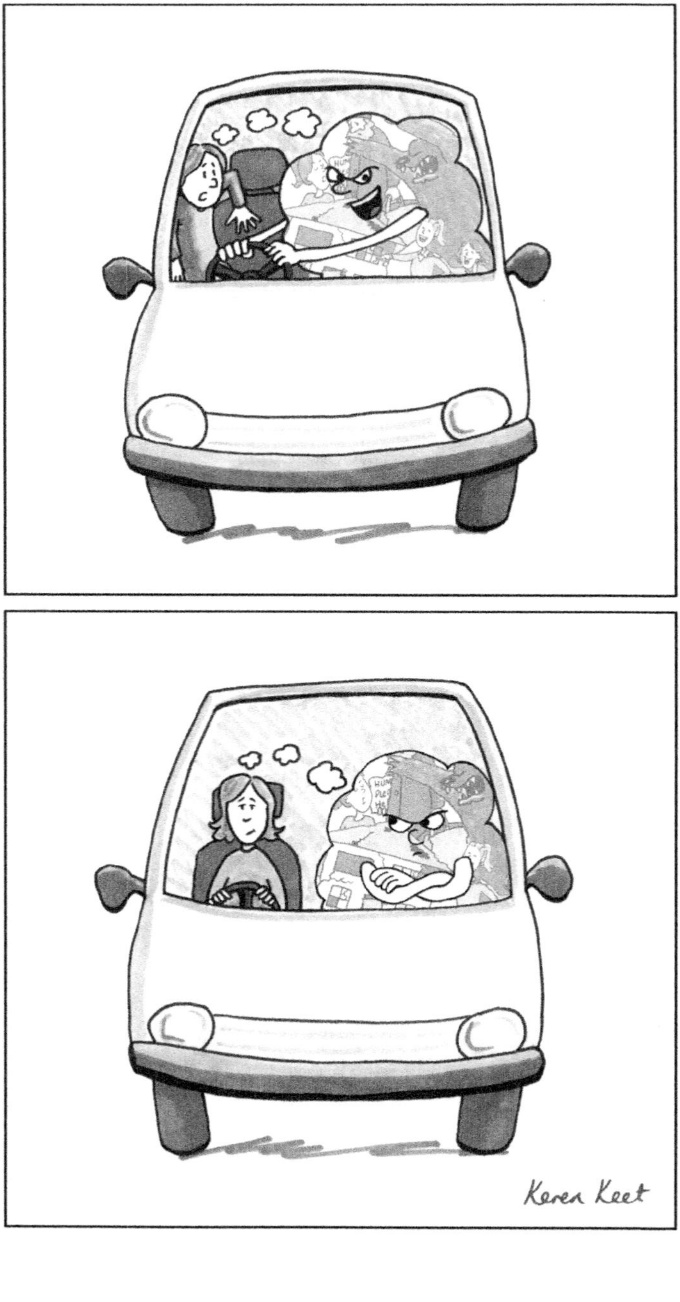
Keren Keet

Natalie used to try quickly to think of something else if disturbing thoughts came into her mind. Once she thought of herself as the driver, she realized that she doesn't need to try to force herself to think about something else (which won't work anyway); she can be confident and honest with herself about what she is thinking and then choose what to focus on.

You are the driver of your car! You can have a relaxed attitude toward the thoughts that come into your mind. They have no power unless you feed them power by running away from them. Look them straight in the eye, and then turn back to the steering wheel and keep driving. The only one who can slip them the keys of the car is you!

We Are Always Anchored

One last thought on this subject:

Avigail was a popular girl who used to constantly be surrounded by a group of friends. She was shocked when her father announced one evening that her family would be moving to a different city. Avigail would need to change schools and make new friends. She would have to get used to so many different things, which would certainly be a challenge.

After the news sunk in, she began to have mixed feelings. On the one hand, she was excited about having a new experience and wondered what her new life would be like. On the other hand, she was nervous about how it would all go and what the challenges would be like. She felt like she was constantly swaying from one emotion to another.

Picture a ship with a heavy anchor. No matter which way the ship sways or drifts in the wind, the anchor will never shift out of place, as it is made of solid material which will not be moved by anything. In the same way, Avigail is anchored in calm and strength. Even though her emotions may sway and change, they will never unhinge her. Even though her moods become unsettled at times and go in different directions, the person she is does not change. Her inner calm and strength do not move, and this gives her, as the "captain of the ship," security — she will not be threatened by any tides or winds that may come. This knowledge helped Avigail to accept her feelings instead of panicking every time she was faced with turmoil.

If you knew that you always have inner security which cannot be swayed by anything, how would you feel?

What Other Teens Have Said About Secret 2

You can accept your feelings.

Even if we are in a simulator, we are still grounded. The floor is still solid under us.

Once you realize that you are normal and stable, you feel more in control and you can move on and do something about it.

Don't ignore what you are feeling. Accept it.

It's amazing to realize that you are still okay even when you don't feel okay!

SECRET 3

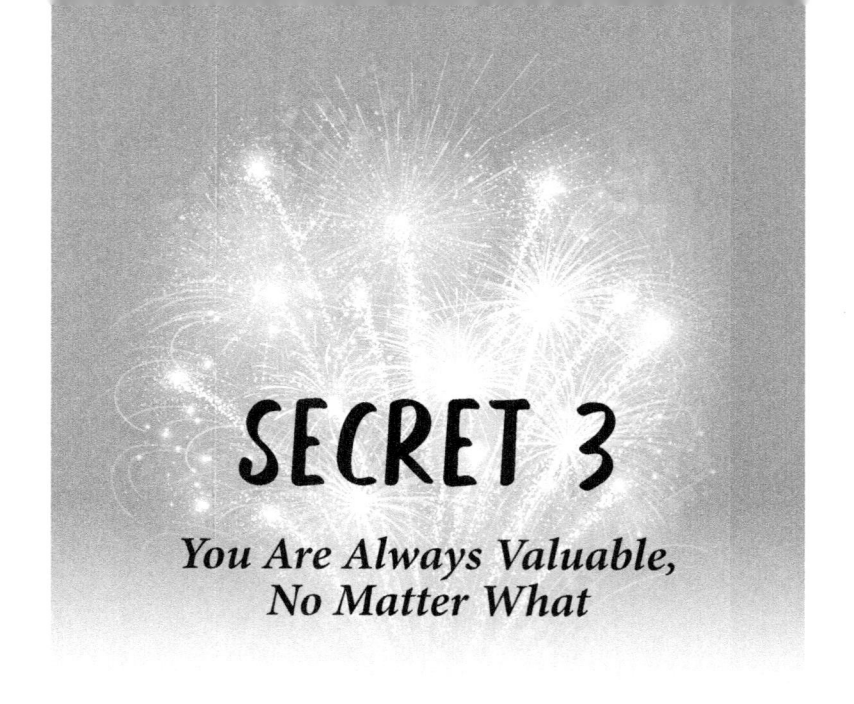

You Are Always Valuable, No Matter What

Where Is the Taste Coming From?

I once decided to try out a new recipe for potatoes. I wanted to check if the potatoes were ready, so I took a fork, speared one, and tasted it. It tasted like dishwashing liquid! I looked at the large tray of potatoes and thought, *Oh no! What now?* But then a thought then struck me: *Are you sure it's the potatoes that have the dishwashing liquid on them? Maybe it's the fork!* Sure enough, I took a new fork, tried another potato, and smiled at the result!

When we "taste" life with the "fork" of insecurity — of not feeling good about ourselves — everything will taste horrible — ourselves, our friends, our family, our schoolwork, any projects we are involved in, and any situations we are dealing with. In this chapter, we will talk about how to put down the "dishwashing liquid fork" and pick up a clean one. We can start to taste life with a clean fork — with a security in ourselves — and boy, does that taste different!

The Wobble Board

A wobble board is a wooden board with a ball attached underneath. The trick is to learn to balance on it. It's a fun thing to try out, but imagine living your life on a wobble board. Imagine carrying out your daily activities on this wobble board. How much energy, time, and focus would be taken up by the simple task of making sure you're not falling off? How much focus would be left to achieve things? How much enjoyment would you have out of the things that you have already?

Goldie's big "rule" was that she had to excel at every test she took. She would stay up late at night studying and had butterflies in her stomach on the morning of a test, whether it was a big or small one. You see, Goldie's "rule" was essentially "You are as good as your grade on a test," so that is why she was so anxious about doing well. Her score would prove whether she was good enough or not! Ironically, the more stressed Goldie got about her scores, the more her mind would freeze during the exams, causing her to get lower grades!

Of course, it is important to achieve in life, and good for Goldie that she took pride in how well she did; that is the way it should be. The point I am making here is that she is valuable before, during, and after the test, no matter which mark she gets. Goldie can step off the wobble board and begin to live with a deep knowledge that she is valuable.

Nowadays, Goldie takes tests from solid ground, and she is amazed to see that this actually *improves* her scores! By now, though, she is happy to receive good grades and feels a sense of achievement, but she knows that no matter what, she is valuable, and there is no need to prove it.

Everyone has "wobble boards" that they can go on: times when they feel insecure about themselves and question whether they are good enough. They feel that unless they prove themselves, they cannot be okay. Here are a few examples of areas in which this manifests itself:

Getting good grades	Being funny	Looking good
Eating well	Making conversation	Being thin
Winning sports games	Being popular	Singing/dancing well

If you knew that you are always valuable and okay, without any conditions, how would you feel? How great would that be? Think about situations in school, at home, or with friends. How different would they be if you would go into them with a guarantee that you are worthy and valuable?

You are good enough because you are you. There's no need to second-guess that! There is always solid ground under you, no matter what mood you are in or what situation you are dealing with. You can step off your wobble board onto solid ground!

Time for an Experiment

Just in case you want proof, here is a simple experiment to test whether you have value:

Check whether your heart is beating. If it is (and I assume it is if you are reading this book . . .), that is absolute proof that you are being created by Hashem in this moment and you are worthy and valuable. Your value is not based on anything on the outside; it is not based on whether you are in a good or bad mood. It just is. It always is!

If you knew that you are always valuable because you are Hashem's child, how would you feel about yourself?

Perfectly Imperfect

Michal often feels very tense and heavy. She feels a lot of pressure to succeed and do everything perfectly. She has to always behave, look, and feel in control and give off the impression to the world that nothing is ever wrong with her.

Michal is in a mindset of perfectionism. She is trying to force herself up a path of perfection, which does not actually exist — life has ups and downs. What is causing Michal to feel this pressure to be prefect? It is coming from Michal's fear of not being good enough and her belief that she will only have value when she is perfect.

I said to Michal, "If you knew that you do not have to be perfect and it is okay to have ups and downs in life, how would you feel?"

The look on her face said it all — she looked so relieved!

We aim to do our best, but this does not mean being perfect.[1] I once saw a great sketch which showed this to me very clearly.

---

1. Tal Ben-Shahar, *The Pursuit of Perfect*.

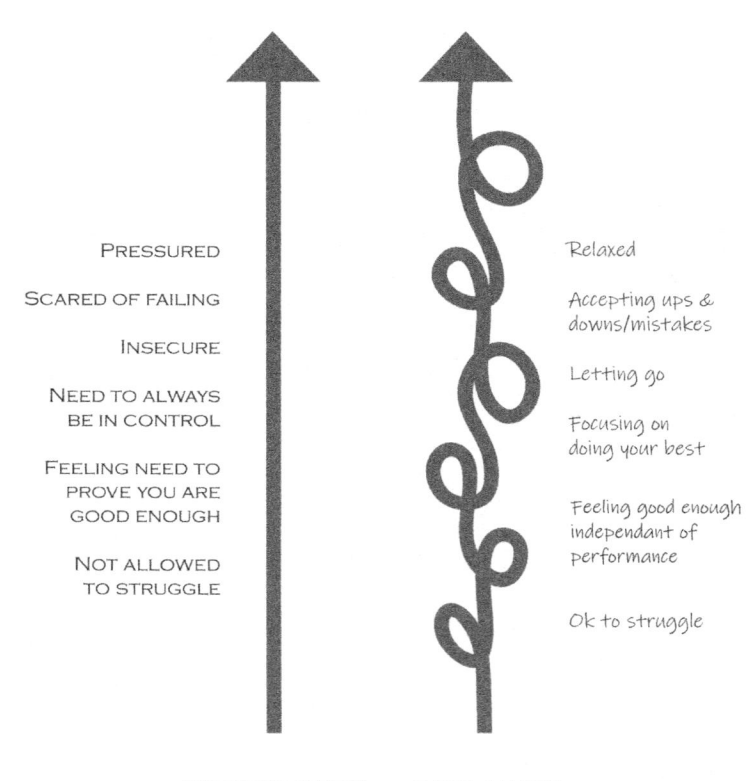

```
        PERFECTIONIST              OPTIMALIST

    PRESSURED                   Relaxed

    SCARED OF FAILING           Accepting ups &
                                downs/mistakes
    INSECURE
                                Letting go
    NEED TO ALWAYS
    BE IN CONTROL               Focusing on
                                doing your best
    FEELING NEED TO
    PROVE YOU ARE               Feeling good enough
    GOOD ENOUGH                 independant of
                                performance
    NOT ALLOWED
    TO STRUGGLE                 Ok to struggle
```

Look at the two lines. You can see that the perfectionism line is straight and rigid. There is no room to move and definitely no room to rest or make a mistake. On this line, Michal will feel like she needs to control things to keep clinging to the line even when she is struggling to do so.

If Michal allows herself to be real and take the optimalist journey, she will still be aiming high in life, but she will accept the reality that sometimes she will look better than other times, sometimes she will feel better than other times, sometimes she will get better marks than other times, and sometimes things in her life will be going more smoothly than other times. She will be able to accept that there will be times when she will be successful and times when she will fail. There will be times when she will make good decisions and times when she will make wrong choices. There will be times when she will be in a good mood and times when she won't feel good. The optimalist path leaves room for all these situations. She will know that she will never fall off the journey and if she dips, she can always reconnect to her goal and take steps toward it again.

Michal can realize that her value is a "backpack" that travels with her on her journey. She is valuable at any point of her journey — the ups, the downs, and anywhere in between. Michal can stop being so scared to fail. She can realize that failure is part of life — everyone gets things wrong at times. Of course, we have to take responsibility for our mistakes, but we do not need to give up on ourselves or lose our belief in our value.

Michal can see that in the optimalism mindset, she can enjoy each step of the journey. It's not just about getting to the top! She can feel achievement with every good choice she makes, every positive step she takes, and every time she gives to another person. In the perfectionism mindset, the only thing that matters is getting to the top. There is no enjoyment in the journey and no appreciation of each achievement, only pressure.

Michal decided that although she will probably, at times, move back into the perfectionism mindset out of habit, she wants to change to an optimalist mindset when she is doing the best she can, allowing for her limitations and mistakes and, most importantly, knowing that she is valuable every step of the way.

Goodbye, Guilt Trips

Let's face it, we all mess up sometimes! We may make wrong decisions, say things that are insensitive, and hurt other people's feelings.

Naomi felt awful. She had been in a very bad mood and had said all sorts of things that she shouldn't have to her parents. She felt stuck and was plagued by a horrible, sinking feeling of guilt.

It felt like all those comments she had said when she was angry were sitting inside her, stuck with no way out. She had seen the hurt look on her mother's face, and every time she pictured it, she felt guilty all over again. She felt totally stuck.

The truth is that Naomi was not stuck, she was at a crossroad. One direction she could go in was to feel like what she did has damaged who she is. Going that way would make her feel like giving up since she has become "infected" by the things she said. The other direction Naomi could go in is one in which she realized that what she did was wrong, but who she is is okay. She could be sorry that she hurt her parents and regret her behavior, but she is on safe ground of always being valuable. This means that she could feel confident enough to look at how she has gone wrong and learn from her mistakes.

Naomi felt much better when she decided to take the latter path. She apologized to her parents but didn't feel like giving up on herself. She could give up her shouting, but not herself! She realized that taking this path not only improved how she felt about herself but also helped her to be in a better mood instead of stewing in guilt. Not a bad package!

What Other Teens Have Said About Secret 3

It's okay to make mistakes

I am still valuable, even when I get things wrong.

I need to do my best, not more.

I used to think that I always have to say the perfect, sensitive thing to people and that I am a terrible person if I ever upset anyone. Now I still aim to be sensitive, but I understand that it is okay not to always get it right! It's such a relief.

SECRET 4

You Can Trust That Hashem Is Pumping You with Awesome Resources

Now for the next secret: One big reason we get into insecure thinking is that we stop trusting. We get stuck in the fear that we have to manage life on our own and that we don't have what it takes. The secret is that Hashem is carrying us through life and He is pumping us with all we need for every moment of our life. We can trust Him, and we can trust ourselves.

The Laptop

Imagine using a high-tech laptop to prop your book up as you are reading it! Doing so means forgetting about the amazing programs installed in the laptop which, when appreciated, can be used for great projects. When we know that the laptop has been programmed by a genius computer programmer, we trust it. We use its programs with excitement and look forward to great outcomes from them. We trust the laptop due to the programs installed on it and the electricity running through it.

In the same way, we are powerful due to the internal workings that Hashem "installs" within us for the life we lead. In each moment, Hashem is sending us wisdom and clarity for whatever it is that we are dealing with. In secure thinking, we are aware of this in the moment, and we feel okay about ourselves, connected to others, and confident in the way we are dealing with situations. Sometimes, insecure thinking clouds our mind, and in those moments we feel unsure of ourselves and of what we are supposed to do.

Tali felt nervous before her interview for a summer job in a school office and was afraid she wouldn't know what to answer if she'd be asked any unexpected questions. Then she remembered about these "programs" that Hashem had installed in her. She could trust the wisdom and energy that Hashem was pumping through her. This really helped Tali to relax and give of her best during the interview. It also helped her stop worrying about any future situations or challenges she would have to deal with in the office if she would be hired. She could trust that she would have the resources to deal with those situations as well.

Just like Tali relaxed when she remembered what Hashem was pumping through her, we can do the same with regard to whatever we are stressed about. Notice how when Tali relaxed, she was able to put her best foot forward during the interview. When we know that we are not the ones controlling things, we can focus better on our part (see chapter 9).

> If you knew that you have amazing resources pumping through you in every moment how would you feel?

What Type of Mirror Are You Looking At?

Seventeen-year-old Elka seemed to be a happy and confident person. Inside herself, however, was a very different picture. She suffered from a lot of anxiety. As far back as she could remember, she never knew what mood her mother would be in at any moment. Sometimes she would be friendly, and sometimes she would explode in anger. In those dark moments, Elka had picked up some thinking of "Don't trust yourself" and "You are not good enough." Like looking through a mirror that creates hilarious distortions, when Elka saw herself, instead of seeing a good, confident person, she saw herself as less than others.

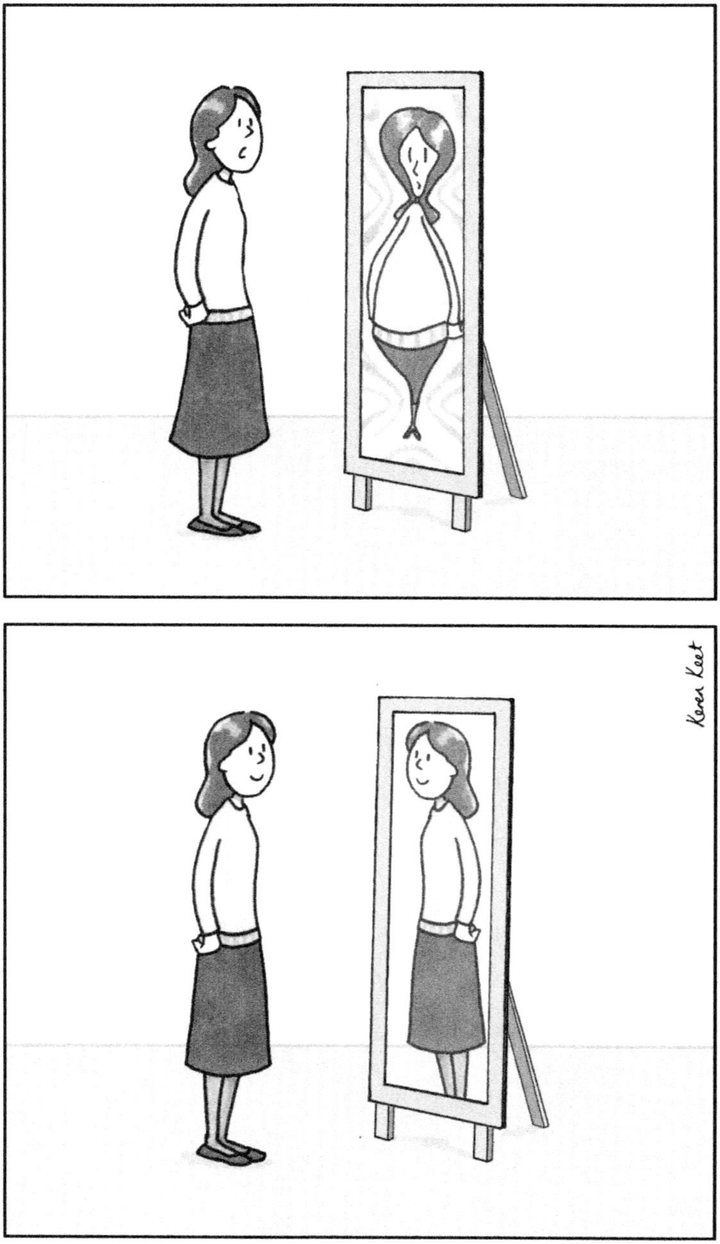

Eventually, Elka began to realize that in every moment, lying patiently and securely beneath her self-critical and scared thinking (which makes her see herself as weak and insecure) is a stream of calm thinking (which helps her see herself as she truly is — capable and worthy). This helped her to laugh when her insecure thinking created insecure images of her. She learned to see herself in a true-to-life way — as a good, capable person. She began to trust, more and more, in the strength, value, and great ideas she has within herself.

Beggar Becomes Millionaire

A rich man quietly slips 1 million dollars into the bag of a sleeping beggar.

The beggar wakes up and shuffles off to try to find some food.

A bystander taps him on the shoulder and tells him to look in his bag.

The beggar discovers that he is a millionaire!

You know those moments when you start to wonder, *Can I really do this? Everyone else seems to have it together, but I definitely don't*? We can call those "moments of self-doubt." I guarantee you that anyone you have met (over age three) has experienced such moments, when their stomach sank and they seriously wondered if they were up to the task set before them. We can begin to view ourselves as beggars and feel that we don't have anything valuable. But when we "look inside our bags" and notice the amazing resources Hashem put inside us, we can discover the value we have and see that we are really "millionaires." Then we can go and "spend some money" by using our resources in our life situations.

Aviva was about to give a speech to her entire school. She had invested much time and effort in writing it and had practiced it a lot, but she was feeling unsure of herself, doubting that she would be able to give the speech in front of so many people. As she was walking up to the podium, her mind whispered, "Don't think you can do this!" She felt like turning around and not giving the speech at all! Then she smiled as she recognized that she was going into "beggar mode." She pictured herself opening her bag and discovering a wad of cash. She realized that Hashem was giving her the ability to give this speech, and she could trust this. Her confidence grew as she remembered the powerful energy Hashem was pumping through her. In the end, her speech went really well, which only proved that she could trust herself to have what she needs for life.

If you knew that you could trust yourself, how would you feel about upcoming projects or situations?

Strong Tree or Dried-Out Leaf?

Shira was dealing with very difficult circumstances. Her older brother was involved in some bad behaviors which sometimes landed him in trouble with the police. Her parents seemed to always be stressed-out and upset. Shira felt like she couldn't deal with it all anymore.

Imagine a dry leaf being blown around by the wind. This is what Shira felt like. She felt out of control, insecure, and easily swayed.

The good news is that Shira is not like a fragile, dry leaf. She is like a strong tree with deep roots embedded in the ground which are constantly supplying the tree with nourishment and hydration.

Winds may blow against it, but it will not be uprooted, due to its sturdy hold on the ground.

This mindset helped Shira to start seeing herself as strong rather than weak. She realized that the roots of her "tree" were so strong that no "storms" could uproot it! Shira became aware that she is always connected to a source of energy that is constantly supplying her with resources. She can trust that she will have the resources to deal with situations as they come up. She can trust herself. Shira also realized that part of her strength is asking for help and support from those who could give that to her.

Sometimes, like Shira, we forget that Hashem gives us the energy, clarity, and ability that we need to deal with our circumstances. We have an inner GPS guiding us through life. We can listen to ourselves. What do we think is best? Do we need to reach out for help from someone? If yes, who? If we trust what we have within ourselves, we will listen out for it a lot more and find great direction when we hear it.

When I was writing this book, I asked a teenager for an example of this idea. Libby told me that she had been taking a math test and her mind had gone blank. She started to panic, but then she allowed herself to relax and wait for the answers to come through. She saw such a difference when she did that. She knew that she did not have to force the answers up from within herself. She had done her bit by studying for the exam, so she could relax and know that the answers would come from a limitless place that she is constantly connected to.

The Right Parking Lot

I once went to Trafford Centre, a huge shopping mall near my home. I got there early, so I easily found a parking spot near the entrance. I left the car to do my shopping, and when I came back two hours later, the parking lot was full of cars, and I had to think hard about where I had parked. I kept retracing my steps, but I just could not find my car! I walked around the entire parking lot three times, getting more and more upset and frustrated as time passed.

I had arranged to pick up my friend's son at one o'clock from his playgroup, and I called her to explain what was happening and asked her if she had any suggestions. She said, "Maybe you are in the wrong parking lot!"

This made me take a step back, as it had not even crossed my mind that I could be looking in the wrong place. When I thought about it, I realized that she could be right and went back up the escalator into the mall. Soon, I discovered another parking lot nearby, and about two minutes later, I was in my car!

As I was driving home, I realized that this is exactly what we can do within our own mind. We can be walking around and around within our own mind trying to find an answer to a problem, getting more and more upset and frustrated as time goes on.

Adina did this whenever she needed to make a decision. She would constantly think about it, going around and around in her own head and driving herself a little crazy! She would ask everyone around her for their opinion and then go around in circles thinking about what they'd said. She felt frustrated and upset.

As Adina began to trust that Hashem will always guide her through her life, she stopped overthinking her decisions and started trusting herself more. Of course, she would ask for advice, but that just helped to point her back in the direction where the answer was really coming from. The answer comes from Hashem, and she did not have to force it. It would surface if she trusted.

The answer comes when we step out of our own limited mind and have the humility to look beyond ourselves and ask Hashem for the answer, which is timeless and far more profound than anything we can force up from within ourselves.

The Faucet

When we moved into our new house, one of the kids went into the kitchen to get a drink of water. They opened the faucet and were surprised to see a stream of brown, muddy water coming out. My husband explained to the children that there had been a buildup of sediment in the pipes while renovations were being done to the house. He suggested that they run the water for a few moments so the dirty water could come out and the clear drinking water could start to flow.

Sometimes this can happen in our mind. We "switch on" our thinking, and "brown, muddy thinking" comes through. We can allow the thoughts to pass, not take them too seriously, and trust that clear thoughts will start to flow soon.

Batya was worried about her mother, who was having some medical tests done. Before she knew it, she began thinking about all the terrible things that could happen and was feeling worse and worse as her thinking continued. Batya was in "murky thinking." She could let it flow without taking it too seriously and trust that "clear thinking" would begin to flow soon, and then, things would look brighter. No matter what the test results would be, her "clear thinking" would give her clarity, hope, and confidence to deal with it.

My friend Zehava and I were once talking on the phone as she was on her way to town on a bus. It was very noisy on the bus, and we had to keep repeating what we were saying since the background noise was preventing us from hearing each other. It was not the smoothest of conversations! Eventually, Zehava said she would call me back when she got off the bus so that we could speak in a quieter environment. She called back a few minutes later and we had a good, clear conversation. It was great that we had acknowledged the background noise so we could have a much better conversation when it was quieter.

Ashira has a lot of "background noise" in her mind when she is hungry. She gets really annoyed with everyone and everything. Ashira can be aware of this pattern. This awareness will give her

THE UNITED STATES OF SPINERICA

FEDERAL RESERVE NOTE

THIS NOTE IS LEGAL TENDER
FOR ALL DEBTS, PUBLIC AND PRIVATE

L 88888888 A

12

ONE DOLLAR

SERIES 2006

WASHINGTON, D.C.

SPIN Story

THE UNITED STATES OF SPINERICA

ONE

IN DOG WE TRUST

SPIN

ONE DOLLAR

tools to deal with it better. If someone asks her a question or for help when she is feeling annoyed, she can say, "Can this wait until I have eaten? I'll speak to you about it soon" since she knows that when her stomach is full, her mind will be quieter, and she will be able to have a much better conversation.

Avoiding "Rush Hour"

During summer vacation, we once traveled to Llandudno, a peaceful seaside resort in Wales, U.K. We timed our return journey so that we could avoid rush hour, enabling us to have a direct, smooth journey home.

Sometimes, it is "rush hour" in our thinking, and our thoughts keep coming, fast and hard. Jumping straight into this thinking can have difficult results. Waiting until it clears enables us to not act on thinking that leads us away from who we are and the way we want to be.

I know that it is not always possible to wait for "rush hour" to pass before dealing with something or someone, and in those cases, we just have to deal with the "traffic" to the best of our ability. Whenever possible, however, we want to be making important decisions and having interactions from the strongest place in ourselves — the place of inner security and clarity.

WHEN WOULD YOU CHOOSE TO TRAVEL??

I once went to the grocery and discovered that there were only a few sorry-looking pears on the shelf. Imagine if I would have given a deep sigh and concluded that this was the end of pears forever! Of course, it was not. I knew and trusted that sometime soon a fresh case of pears would be delivered to the store and I would be able to enjoy them. I just needed a little patience!

Trusting that freshness will come when we are bogged down can give us hope.

The Three-Seater Couch

Pearli felt like she had a tug-of-war going on inside her. She often felt strong anger and negative feelings toward her parents. On the other hand, she knew that they cared about her, and she had to admit (although begrudgingly sometimes) that she cared about them too. When she was in a bad mood, what she knew deep down disappeared. On the other hand, she could not deny how she felt at times.

I think of it as a three-seater couch. Pearli is sitting in the middle. What she feels is on one side, and what she knows deep down is on the other. There is enough room for both! Pearli can feel anger *and* know how much she really cares about her parents — at the same time.

Our Inner Voice Is Always Playing

We all have a voice inside us that is confident, calm, and clear and helps us to connect to those around us. It is our GPS which guides us in whatever we need to do. Sometimes we hear that voice clearly. These are the moments when we feel confident, at ease, relaxed, connected to others, and hopeful. We know what we need, and we know how to go about getting it. Other times, our thoughts may create a lot of noise around this voice, and we can't hear it. This in no way means that our inner voice has gone anywhere. It is still there, and once the background noise stops, we will hear that voice clearly again.

What Other Teens Have Said About Secret 4

> Trust in yourself and in the fact that there are lots of amazing tools that you can use.

> Hashem has given us everything, and it's all in our pockets

> I like realizing that only if we reach out to Hashem can we receive help from Him.

> I don't have to be in control of every little thing.

> You can tackle anything you need to in life.

> It's great to realize that we can hand things over to Hashem. That relaxes me.

> I don't always find it easy, but I feel more confident when I realize that Hashem is running the show.

SECRET 5

You Always Have the Power to Choose

If I ask you, "How powerful is a remote-control car?" you might look at me and say, "Not powerful at all! The person who is holding the remote has all the power. If they decide to pull the lever back, the car moves back; if they push the lever forward, the car moves forward; and if they press the button, the car flips over."

Each one of us has a "remote control." The question is, who is holding it?

Shiffy was behaving in a very reactive way toward her family members, particularly her siblings. If anyone would touch her things, she would yell and hit them. If anyone made any negative comment to her, she would shoot back a stronger one.

Shiffy had thrown her remote control outside of herself. She had allowed herself to become a "remote-control car" and be controlled by people on the outside. It was as if she was telling other people that they could decide how she acts. If they do what she wants, she will be in a good mood. If they speak nicely to her, she will speak nicely back.

Shiffy wondered why she felt so insecure. We have the answer: she needed to take her remote control back! She needed to realize that she can decide what type of day she will have and how she will respond. She has the control.

With time, Shiffy began to learn that she has a whole range of choices of how she can respond. She can't choose or control her siblings' or parents' actions, but when it comes to her response, she is queen. No one is in control of how she chooses to react but she.

Why should she be able to control me like this?
Great! Now I've got my control back!
Karen Keet

If Shiffy feels annoyed about something one of her siblings does or says, she can be honest with herself about the fact that she is bothered. She can then decide what the best way of dealing with the situation is. She doesn't necessarily have to sit there and let them annoy her; she can choose to ask them to stop in a nice way or leave the room. This is Shiffy holding her remote. She is in control. She can choose.

If Shiffy feels annoyed and thinks she has no choice how to act, she has thrown the remote to the people around her, and they will have lots of fun with it! It wouldn't be much fun for Shiffy, though. Taking the remote back is the best way for her to feel in control of herself and focus on finding the best solution in each situation.

Home Sweet Home

Sometimes it feels like the people or situations around us are taking our power away. We forget that we have choices. We start to react and get stuck in what is going on around us.

Debbie often felt like this at home. She has a sister with special needs who takes up a lot of her parents' attention. Debbie began to forget about her own power and choices and was constantly focused on her sister's needs and moods. She was always trying to make the situation at home less stressful, and she stopped looking after herself and focusing on her own life. Although she didn't want to admit it, she would often feel angry and resentful toward her sister for causing the situation.

The good news is, Debbie *does* have her own power — she simply forgot that she is allowed to use it! She forgot that she is her own person, not just an extension of everyone around her. When she loses sight of her choices, she loses sight of her power.

I like to think of it as each person having their own house.

Your choices & decisions

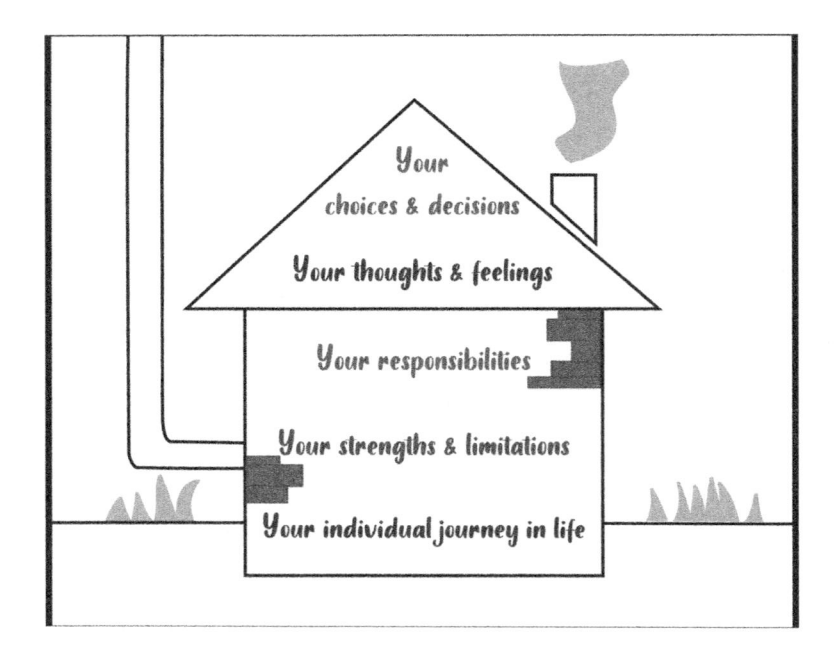

Your thoughts & feelings

Your responsibilities

Your strengths & limitations

Your individual journey in life

Each of us has such a "house." As you can see, there is a pipe at the side of the house. Just like a house has gas and water pipes which deliver a flow of energy to the house, so too, each of us has a "pipe" that comes to our house with everything we need for each moment of our life. There is courage, strength, wisdom, and a clear idea of how to deal with what is going on outside of our house.

When we are "home," we feel focused and trust ourselves to have the ability to cope with whatever we have to deal with. We catch the energy. Those are the moments when we feel confident, focused, hopeful, and trusting of ourselves. We are aware of how we feel about things and focused on our choices regarding how to respond to what we can't control, i.e., how to respond to everything that is going on outside of our house, such as other people's moods, our family situation, where we live, a flight being canceled, or a big exam that is coming up. We can always control our own house — we can control how we choose to respond to the things that we can't control.

When we feel hopeless and disempowered, we have stepped out of what we can control and into what we can't control. We have stepped out of our house and onto the street.

The good news is that our house is portable. It goes with us wherever we go, no matter whom we are with and what we are dealing with. We always have a powerful place to go to in ourselves where we can catch our strength and make choices.

We Are Royal by Birth

In England, where I live, we have a royal family. When a royal baby is born, even before they have done anything to deserve it, they receive royal care and treatment. They haven't *earned* it. It is coming to them because they have been born royal.

Our house is not something that needs to be earned, it is something that we were granted when we were born because we are Hashem's children. We always have the right to be valued, we always have the ability to choose, and we always have the right to a certain level of respect. Everyone does!

What Are We Hanging on the Walls of Our House?

More good news! We get to choose which slogans or pictures we hang on the walls of our house. We can choose what mindset we want to live by. Here are a few ideas you could "hang up" which can help you to connect with your inner confidence:

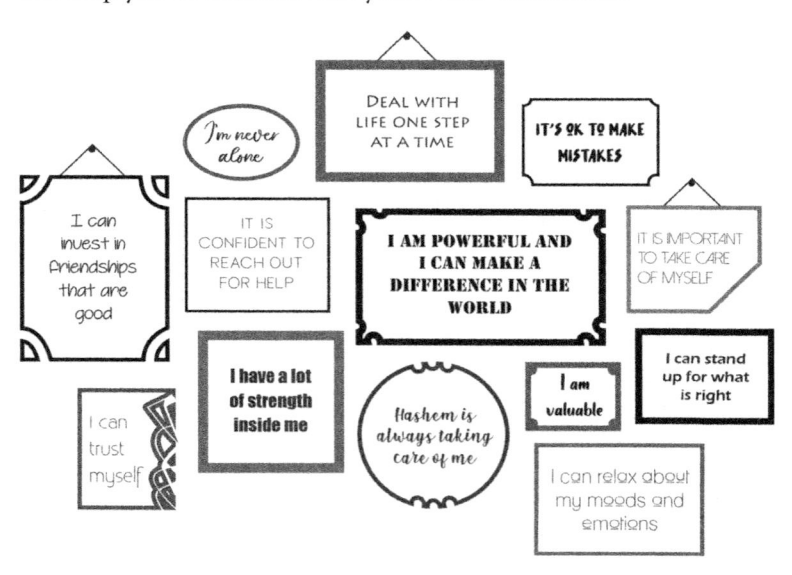

- I'm never alone
- Deal with life one step at a time
- It's ok to make mistakes
- I can invest in friendships that are good
- It is confident to reach out for help
- I am powerful and I can make a difference in the world
- It is important to take care of myself
- I can trust myself
- I have a lot of strength inside me
- Hashem is always taking care of me
- I am valuable
- I can stand up for what is right
- I can relax about my moods and emotions

Taking Care of Our House

The owner of a Rolls-Royce likely takes very good care of their car. They consistently clean and polish it and make sure all the parts of the car are regularly serviced and in good working order. After all, it is worth around four hundred thousand dollars!

Each of us is a "Rolls-Royce" since we have been created by Hashem. When you appreciate the value that you have, you will be able to invest in yourself and take care of yourself at least as well as one cares for a Rolls-Royce, if not better!

Here are some ideas of how you can do so:

> GET SOME SLEEP! I know its not always easy but get to bed at a reasonable time
>
> EXPRESS YOURSELF Through music, writing, dancing
>
> EXERCISE Find a way to exercise that you enjoy e.g: walking, swimming, aerobics
>
> SOCIALIZE Reach out to others, meet up with friends
>
> APPRECIATE NATURE See a stunning sunset, scenery, flowers, animals
>
> KEEP INSPIRED Listen or learn things which inspire you to be your best

The Tennis Game

Tova had been looking forward to going away with her family to Bournemouth in the south of England for a few nights during her midwinter vacation. It took her parents a while to get the car packed up, and they needed to make two stops before beginning the journey to their vacation spot. Avi, Tova's six-year-old brother, was getting frustrated about how long it was taking to leave. He let everyone know about it by grumbling, which soon became full-fledged screaming. Tova was squashed in the back of the car next to Avi, whose crying was piercing her eardrums. All her excitement and hope for a great vacation began to drain away, and she began to feel angry and disappointed. She felt that Avi had spoiled the vacation before they had even started the journey!

We can understand Tova's frustration with Avi, but the good news is that Tova did not need to give up on an enjoyable vacation because of the atmosphere in the car. The way I see it is that Tova was at "match point." I will explain.

During a game of table tennis, the two players are obviously both trying to win. If they have an equal number of points, it is called "match point." It is an exciting moment. Whichever player scores wins the game!

Tova was playing in the "game of life." In that moment of her frustration, disappointment, and desire to give up and descend into a bad mood for the rest of the trip, she was at "match point" — she was at the exciting moment of opportunity to score and win the game. She could decide that even though she was bothered, she could choose to do the best she could not to let that spoil her vacation.

The truth is, we are always at "match point" in life. We always have the opportunity to make choices. Choices can be about the most mundane matters, such as choosing the color of a new sweater or which route to take to the store, or it can be about more significant things like which friends are good for us or how to speak respectfully even when we are annoyed. If we think honestly, we'll realize that our choices are the only area in life that we are really in control of. This is where our inner force is channeled. We operate in this world as people, rather than machines which are programmed to run automatically. We breathe life and energy into what we do and the steps we take.

We Matter

Imagine if the president of the United States would be faced with a decision, and he'd say, "It doesn't matter what I do!" That would be crazy. He is the president; of course, what he does matters. He is an extremely valuable member of society, and therefore, what he does absolutely matters.

When we realize our value, we realize that our decisions matter. What we say, what we do, and whom we spend our time with all matter. They matter, because we matter.

Parenting Classes for Dolphins?

Dolphins are known to be cruel to their young. What would you say if I told you that I was planning to organize parenting classes for dolphins? I think you would laugh, and for good reason! You know that dolphins will be dolphins and will always act in the way that is natural to them. We will never be able to change that.

As human beings, however, we have free choice, which raises us into a totally separate category from animals and allows us to grow and transform our natural tendencies.

If you knew that you are always free to choose how to respond to things, what would this knowledge give you?

New Moment, New Choice

I am writing this paragraph at 4:47 p.m. on Thursday, September 26, 2020. What would you say to me if I told you that this is always going to be the time and date from now on? I assume you would laugh. That is, of course, ridiculous. The next minute will be 4:48, tomorrow will be Friday, next month will be October, and next year will be 2021.

The same way that it is an absolute given that time moves on, so too, there are always new opportunities. We are *never* stuck and can always move from wherever we are.

Imagine if you took a wrong turn on a trip and your GPS announced, "You have gone off the route and are stuck here forever!" We smile at this because we know there will always be the option to get on the right track from wherever we are.

Ruti was trying to behave well in school, which did not come naturally to her. She had previously gotten into a lot of trouble in school, and the classroom was definitely not her favorite place to be. But recently, she had been behaving much better, speaking more politely to the teachers and trying to complete her work.

One day, she was in a particularly bad mood and said something very inappropriate to one of the teachers, who got extremely offended. Ruti felt like giving up. She had been doing so well and now she had messed everything up. She felt very stuck and like there was no point in trying anymore.

Ruti had taken a "wrong turn." Instead of acting respectfully, she had done the opposite. There is always the opportunity for her to "recalculate" and find a new way forward from her failure. She is never going to be "stuck there forever" unless she tells herself that and then believes it!

Gratitude Is the Way to Go

Gratitude is another area in which we have an opportunity to choose.

Research shows that gratitude helps people have good friendships, improves moods, helps people sleep and be physically healthy, improves self-esteem, and helps deal with life situations better.[2] Quite a good package, don't you think?

I know it can feel more fun sometimes to complain about what is going wrong in our life and how difficult things are. And there is a time for expressing this. At some point, though, we hit a crossroad. Are we going to focus on what is wrong, or are we going to focus on what is right? Are we going to constantly think about what is hard or also consider what is going smoothly?

Gratitude does not mean ignoring whatever is difficult, it means choosing to focus on what we can appreciate in ourselves, our life, or others. There are always things that are going well, and there are always things that are not. What are we zooming in on? Which parts of our life are we filming and taking pictures of? We get to choose that.

---

2. Dr. Robert A. Emmons of the University of California and Dr. Michael E. McCullough of the University of Miami, "Counting Blessings Versus Burdens: An Experimental Investigation of Gratitude and Subjective Well-Being in Daily Life."

Do You Need a Boost?

So, in summary, we don't control what happens outside of our house, but we always have control over what comes *from* our house. We choose how we respond. Here are some ideas of things to do when you feel that you need a boost. Choose whichever ones work best for you.

Gratitude list

Do something you enjoy

Journal

Do deep breathing to calm yourself down

Listen to music or to an inspirational talk

Talking to someone who can understand or help you

Exercise

Davening

Helping someone

What Other Teens Have Said About Secret 5

> Everyone is unique; we all add to the world in our own way.

> We always have control; it's up to us to use it!

> I like to think of that 'table tennis shot.' It helps me to focus myself and choose well even when I am really annoyed!

> I didn't realize how often I feel out of control. I liked learning that I can make choices about the things I can't control. I feel stronger.

SECRET 6
No One Can Control You

"Okay, I get what you mean about my mood coming from my mind," admitted Gila. "But what about when my parents act in a way that is unfair or my teachers yell at me? If I get upset or angry about this, it's coming from *them*, not from my mind. They make me annoyed! It has nothing to do with me."

We can understand what Gila is saying. It can definitely feel like our feelings about other people and their behavior come from them, not from our thinking. But the truth is, our feelings can only ever come from our thinking in the moment.

Have a look at the diagram below which shows how secure and insecure thinking create the way we experience our relationships. Notice how Gila can feel such different feelings toward the same people depending on which "floor" she is on within herself. Other people's behavior can never trap her into insecure thinking. No matter what, there is always the potential for her to shift to secure thinking.

Confident
Relaxed **Decisive** IN CONTROL
Respect of self and others
Connected Self-value

Secure Thinking
Insecure Thinking

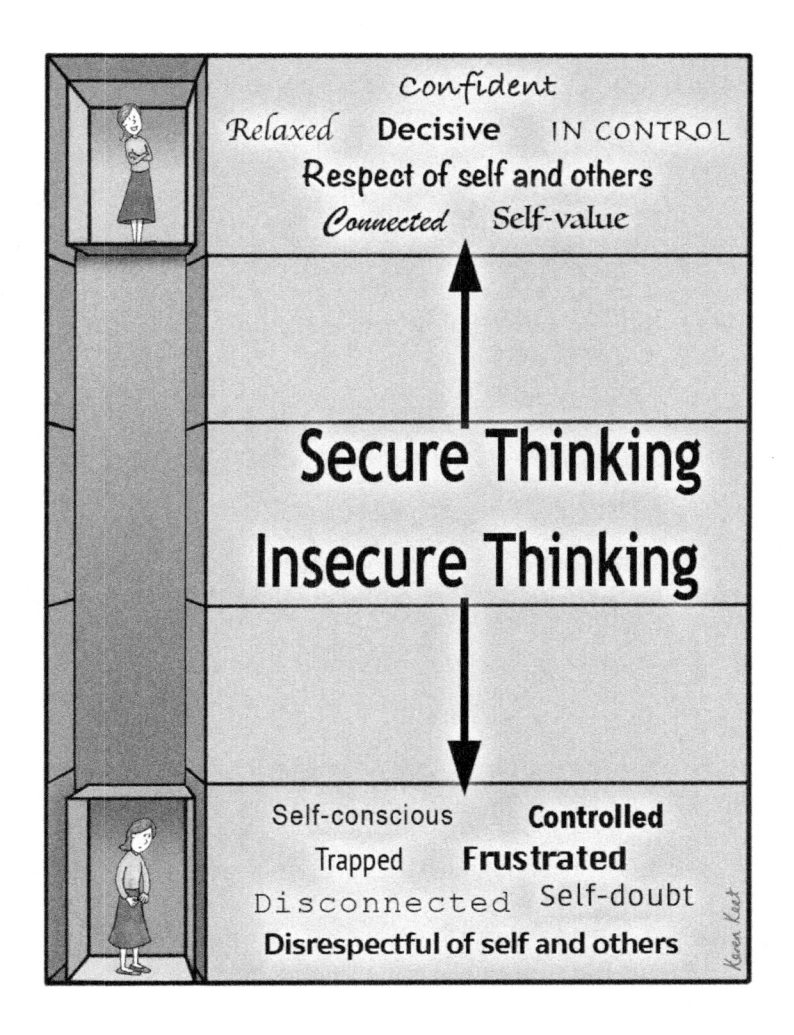

Self-conscious **Controlled**
Trapped **Frustrated**
Disconnected Self-doubt
Disrespectful of self and others

When we realize this, instead of feeling trapped in how we are experiencing a relationship or allowing ourselves to be controlled by the other person's behavior, we have the potential to find a completely different way of experiencing the situation and therefore dealing with it. This does not mean that people always behave appropriately. It means that there is a space between their behavior and how we experience it and what we choose to do about it. All the levels are open to us, no matter what mood the other person is in or how they are acting.

Dina walked past a classmate in the street, and the classmate ignored her. Dina could go to a low floor of insecure thinking about this situation and start to think that there is something wrong with her or worry that she has offended this girl. Alternatively, she could experience *exactly the same thing* and look at it from a high floor, where she accepts her feelings about it but still feels relaxed and confident.

In this chapter, we will discuss common ways in which we can start to slip into insecure thinking and therefore experience our relationships from lower floors in the building. More importantly, we'll talk about what we need to know or do to get back onto the higher floors.

We said in chapter 5 that we each have our own "house." We are confident and secure when we are home and are catching the exquisite energy that Hashem is sending us. But when we jump into someone else's house, we feel unsure and unfocused. We lose sight of our own power and start to feel controlled by the other person.

"My sister Shevy takes me out of my 'house,'" claimed Miriam. "She is always saying mean comments to me, telling me what to do, and driving me crazy."

Notice how Miriam looks in her house compared to how she looks when she jumps into Shevy's — in other words, when she allows Shevy's comments to control her mood and runs around doing things for Shevy to keep her happy even when it doesn't feel right for her, or when she is focusing on Shevy's life instead of taking responsibility for her own.

Miriam's House *Shevy's House*

Though we can understand Miriam's thinking that she can be pulled out of her house, the good news is that this is actually *impossible*. We actually have to *step out* of our house in order to feel insecure. If Miriam focuses on herself and has a confident attitude toward Shevy, no matter what Shevy does or says, she cannot pull her out. Each house has its own central heating system. Shevy cannot switch Miriam's off! The only way Miriam will feel "cold" is if she steps out of her house — out of being connected to herself — and onto Shevy's "doorstep."

So let's say Shevy bosses Miriam around. Miriam can either say, "I feel annoyed about what Shevy did" and accept that, which is staying in her house, or she can say, "Shevy *made me* annoyed," which is letting Shevy control her. If Miriam stays in her own house, focused on what she feels and the choices she can make, she will feel the warmth of her own "central heating system" by feeling confident, focused, and grounded. As soon as she starts getting stuck in Shevy's house, she will start to feel insecure, unfocused, and out of control.

When I received answers to my questionnaire for teenagers, one of the biggest things that struck me was how many of the teenagers spoke about struggles they have with other people, mainly siblings and friends. Let's use this house analogy to shine light on different ways that we can struggle in relationships and without realizing it, allow others to control us.

Comparing to Others

Tehilla always felt like she was competing with her younger sister Tzippy. Tzippy is the type of person who excels at everything she does. She achieves great grades and is really popular. Tehilla always felt like a second-class citizen next to her and was blind to the fabulous qualities that she herself has — she is outgoing, kind, and creative, but these are not the type of qualities that would show up on her report card! Tehilla was unconfident and unsure of herself and was constantly comparing herself to Tzippy. Every decision she made or comment that someone made to her was judged by whether it would make her feel silly next to Tzippy. She was constantly on guard, particularly around Tzippy and her friends. It was really affecting her life. She was not living in her own house; she was living in Tzippy's house since she was constantly trying to prove herself to Tzippy, focusing on what she would think and worrying that she was not good enough in her eyes.

Tehilla had the opportunity to step back into her own house, to focus on her own good *middos* (traits), artistic talent, and ability to understand others, instead of focusing on Tzippy's strengths. If she would do this, instead of feeling unsure of herself and the need to prove that she is as good as Tzippy, she would know that she is good enough being herself. The discussion would be over, and Tehilla's constant excursions to Tzippy's house would stop.

Tehilla could begin to make decisions, receive grades on her tests, and have social interactions in a relaxed way, from her own house. She could know that no outside circumstances can diminish her value. She could be living life from *her* house, with a solid recognition of her right to have value and worth because Hashem created her. This is available to her in her house. She would no longer have to look outside herself for proof that she is okay, that she is good enough. She would know that she is.

Once Tehilla was able to accept herself, she became more creative in the ways she used her strengths and started giving art lessons to girls who were struggling in school as she had, using her traits of patience and sensitivity to help them. She also noticed that people tend to feel comfortable around her and trust her. She stopped seeing her limitations as failures and instead viewed them as something she could use to help herself, but only if she is "home."

The same way that all the houses on a block are unique, each built in a different shape or with a different-colored front door, so too, each person is unique.

You have your own purpose in this world, and no one can or will fulfill it for you. It is the purpose of your creation. I need to focus on mine and confidently allow others to do theirs. The fact that no two people — even identical twins — look exactly alike reflects the reality that no two people *are* exactly alike, and therefore, everyone has something different to offer to the world.[3]

If you knew that you can be confident to be yourself, how would you feel?

---

3. *Brachos* 58a.

Take Your Key Back

Daniella always felt like she was an outsider in school. The louder, more outgoing girls in her class seemed to be given more importance, and she always felt like she was one step behind.

With time, Daniella realized that importance has absolutely nothing to do with how many funny comments she can make, how loudly she speaks, or whether she is surrounded by a group of girls. Importance has to do with *her value*. She realized that her more reserved personality is not a problem; it does not make her less than others. She can encourage herself to be a little more sociable at times, to stretch herself to enhance her social life rather than just staying home and reading a book, but in no way does she have to prove her right to belong. She is important, and nothing can change that.

I was once about to leave my house to give a talk and was looking all over the house for my car keys. I just couldn't find them! It was getting late, and I was running around looking for them. Absentmindedly, I put my hand in my coat pocket and… you guessed it! There were my keys. They had been in my pocket all along while I was looking for them everywhere else!

I realized that this is what we do in life. We look outside of ourselves for recognition of our value and permission to be confident in who we are, and meanwhile, the keys have been in our pocket the whole time! The keys to valuing ourselves, appreciating how special we are, and living our life in a way that reflects this have never actually gotten lost.

Remember the key to your house is in your pocket…

Daniella realized that she could take the key back into her own hands. She stopped throwing it to the world and letting them decide whether she has value, importance, and approval. It is hers. She is now committed to constantly accepting herself.

It was amazing for Daniella to discover that the key to her own house, her own feeling of value and importance, was in *her* pocket. Previously, she had been dependent on the approval of other people. She'd felt like the key was in *their* hands to decide whether she was good enough, and it was a scary position to be in. She'd felt like she had no control. If others would talk to her, smile at her, or approve of her, she felt good, and if they'd ignore her, she felt bad. After her realization, however, she knew that she could not get "locked out" because the key would always be in her pocket.

The Transparent Dome: Dealing with Criticism

Riva's older sister always seemed to have something not nice to say to her. She was always telling her what was wrong with what she was wearing and making comments if she ever slipped up. It was really getting to her!

After learning that she has her own "house" which is secure and cannot be attacked by anything or anyone on the outside, Riva began to picture a transparent dome over herself and her sister's comments sliding off the side of it.[4] Riva could stay secure and safe inside it. With time, she began to see the innocence in her older sister's judgments and criticism and actually felt sorry for her that the only way she could feel good about herself was by putting down those around her.

---

4. B. Bays, *The Journey for Kids*.

Now, I just want to make something clear. Sometimes we do need others to point out ways that we have to improve or change. But first, we have to clarify two things:

1) Does the person have a right to criticize me? (Is it a parent, teacher, good friend, or someone else who is important in my life?)

2) Are they putting me down *as a person* with their criticism or just pointing out something I need to work on?

The point is to graciously accept constructive criticism and at the same time know that this does not chip away at our value. We are who we are. Such an attitude will open up a better path for us. (Remember the crossroads in "Secret 3," page 44.)

86

The Snap Game: Focusing on What We Can Change

I was once playing the game Snap with my daughter. Each player has a pile of cards and gets a turn to put down the top card next to the top card of the other player. When they match, the first to shout "Snap!" gets both piles of cards. We both finished our piles, and there were no more opportunities for "Snap!" i.e., no matching cards. I said that I would shuffle my pile and we would play again. My daughter asked me if she should reshuffle hers as well. I replied, "There's no need. Even if I only shuffle mine, the game will be different."

It then struck me that it is the same with relationships. If there is bullying, criticism, or any other type of unhealthy "game" going on between two people, and one makes a change on their side, the "game" will automatically change. If one stands up and decides to act with confidence, to take responsibility for their behavior or to stop taking things personally, the relationship will change even if the other person continues with the same behavior. (With time, it often happens that the other person's behavior will also change.)

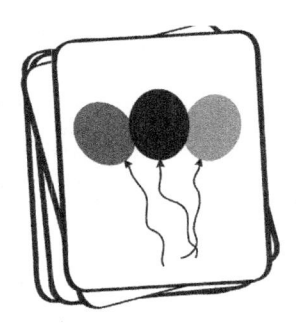

SHUFFLING YOUR CARDS CHANGES THE WHOLE GAME!

Gali was having trouble in school. She had certain teachers whom she did not get along with, and she let them know about it!

It became a power struggle, and she would often get into trouble, sometimes in an unfair way. Gali was very frustrated and dreaded going to school. She could not see how things could be different if teachers were still going to be in her school!

Once Gali began to realize that she could change the whole situation by changing her side, she began to wonder if things could get better. That did not mean the problem was all her fault — her teachers did act unfairly sometimes — but she could take her power back by choosing how she would act. She knew that if she stayed confident in herself and focused on her own ability to choose to act well, she would not slip into the old pattern of getting into fights with her teachers.

The next time she was told off for talking during class, she stayed relaxed and simply stopped talking instead of feeling threatened by the teacher and answering back, which was usually where the problems started. Another time, she was bothered by an unfair punishment the teacher gave to the whole class, and whereas normally, she would have argued aggressively, now she was able to take a step back. She decided to go speak to the teacher after class and tell her respectfully what was bothering her, and she was pleasantly surprised at how different the ensuing conversation was compared to any previous ones!

Gali had shuffled her "cards" — she was no longer coming from a nervous, angry, and insecure place but rather a confident, relaxed, and respectful place. The whole "game" was totally different.

When we focus on the behavior of others, we don't feel powerful because we don't have control over that. When we zone in on ourselves and how we want to deal with it, we will feel our power again.

Putting the Roof on Our House: Making Boundaries

Tova found it very difficult to say no. Actually, that is an understatement. Tova *never* said no. If someone would ask her for help, she would say yes right away, without even hearing the end of the sentence! She would often find herself stressed-out since she felt she had to do things that didn't feel right to her.

Sometimes, a troubled girl in her class, Zlaty, would call Tova very late at night and tell her disturbing things that she felt uncomfortable hearing. Tova would stay on the phone as long as Zlaty wanted. She would then find it very hard to fall asleep and the next day in school would space out during class, thinking of all the things Zlaty had said.

Tova needed to learn to put boundaries in place. She needed to learn to listen to herself about what she was comfortable with and what she wasn't and to be confident to stick to what she felt was right for her. She needed to risk being rejected by Zlaty if she told her what she wanted. She needed to find a sensitive and confident way to tell Zlaty what time she could call until and that she was not comfortable to talk about certain issues, so perhaps Zlaty should find an adult to speak to about those issues. But Tova did not believe she could do it. She thought she would feel so uncaring and guilty. But she was determined to try and was amazed at how confident she felt after her decision.

I think of boundaries like the roof of a house. A house can remain standing without a roof, but all the warmth goes out of it and it lacks security and protection. Boundaries create security. Although they are sometimes difficult to put in place, they are well worth the effort.

If we realize how precious we are, we will realize that we are worth taking care of. We'll make sure not to let ourselves be taken advantage of and stop focusing more on caring for others than on caring for ourselves. We will realize that everyone deserves to be cared for and respected, and we are part of that "everyone."

Trusting no one, or everyone

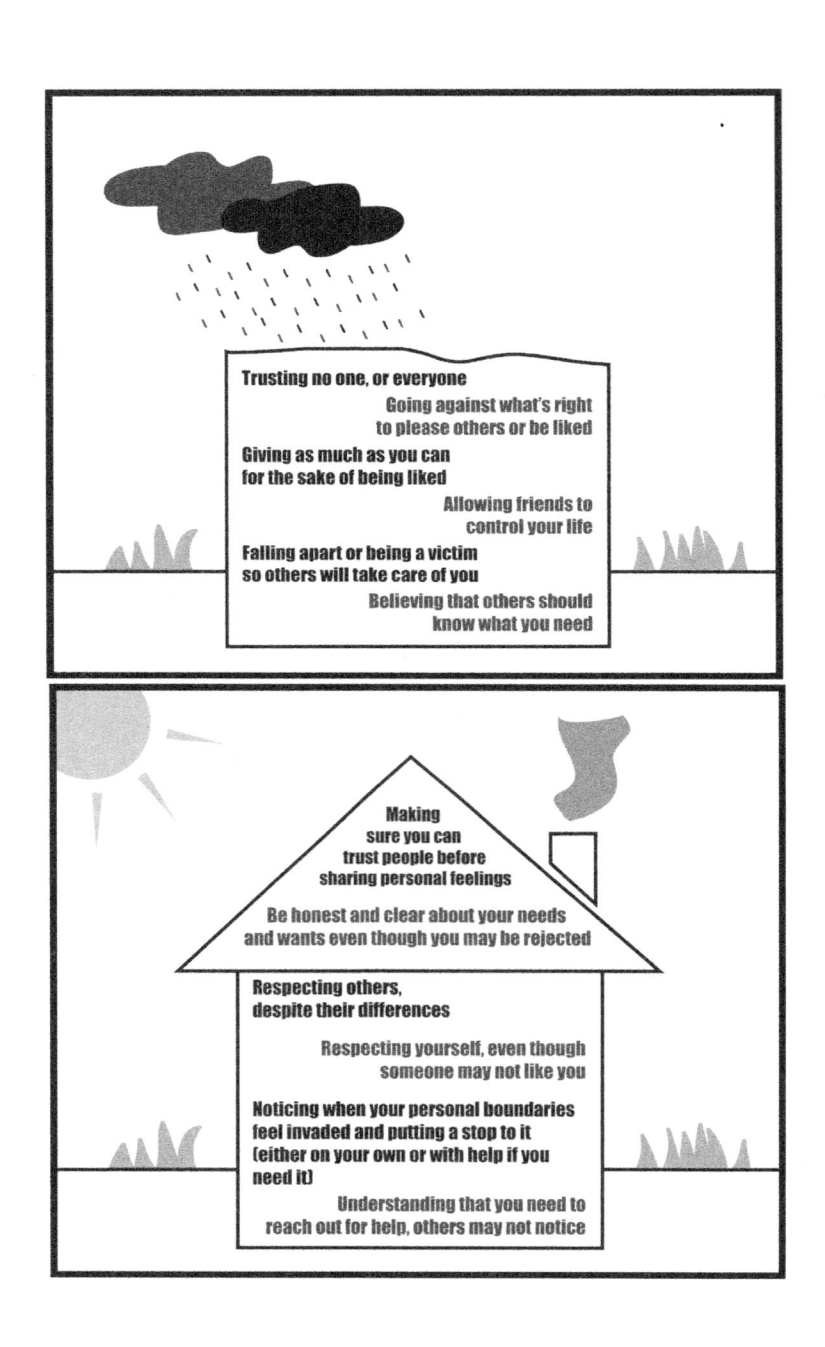

Going against what's right to please others or be liked

Giving as much as you can for the sake of being liked

Allowing friends to control your life

Falling apart or being a victim so others will take care of you

Believing that others should know what you need

Making sure you can trust people before sharing personal feelings

Be honest and clear about your needs and wants even though you may be rejected

Respecting others, despite their differences

Respecting yourself, even though someone may not like you

Noticing when your personal boundaries feel invaded and putting a stop to it (either on your own or with help if you need it)

Understanding that you need to reach out for help, others may not notice

Staying Home: How to Manage When Those We Care About Are Struggling

Malka's good friend Penina was having an extremely hard time. There was a difficult situation going on at home, and she would get into very intensely sad moods. Malka found herself thinking about Penina a lot of the time. She felt guilty whenever she was having a good time with her other friends since she knew that Penina was probably feeling awful. In short, Malka felt responsible for Penina. Every time Malka mentioned that Penina should talk to an adult who could help her, she got a mouthful of angry words, and then Malka would feel like she had to deal with helping Penina herself. She kept jumping into Penina's "house" and trying to tidy it up for her.

Malka realized that going back to her house meant that she absolutely still cared about Penina but she needed to stop trying to solve her problems. Only Penina could do that. Her role as a friend was to tell someone who could help Penina, like a teacher or an older sibling, even at risk of Penina being upset at her. She could show that she cares, daven for her, visit her, and be sensitive in the way she speaks to her, but only Penina could tidy up her own house; Malka could not do it for her.

Malka could not believe the difference in how she felt when she stopped getting stuck in Penina's house. She realized that caring about Penina means staying in her own house and giving from there when it is appropriate. There is a space between Penina's house and her house. Malka had been feeling like if she did not give everything to Penina, Penina would have nothing. She had mistakenly thought that Penina's strength comes through her. But now she knew that Penina has her own pipe directly from Hashem to her, giving her what she needs for her life, and Malka has what she needs for her life.

Still, Malka felt guilty at first. She was so used to putting Penina first in everything she did and ignoring her own needs. With time and guidance, though, she took an important step back into her own house. Malka saw that as she began to step back from this heavy responsibility, she began to enjoy the times she visited Penina more. She realized that just like she was not responsible for breathing for Penina as a caring friend, she was not responsible for dealing with her life either. She started to see strength in Penina which she had never noticed before and felt more hopeful that Penina could access this power and improve. She stopped feeling that any recovery Penina could experience would need to come through her. She saw that Hashem has many different messengers, and she would happily carry out her tasks and leave the rest to others.

> If you knew that you can care about others without taking responsibility for their problems, how would you feel? Is there anything you would do differently in any of your relationships?

Sari was in a different situation, but she had similar feelings. She suffered from an illness that meant that she often had to be rushed to the hospital. She felt so guilty about how her illness affected the other members of her family and felt responsible for their struggles.

Stepping back into her own house meant that Sari understood that her illness does affect her parents, siblings, and friends but she does not have to feel heavy about it. Looking at the situation from her house means that she can know that each of the people she cares about has an independent pipe coming to them directly from Hashem, and she does not need to control how they deal with things. She realized that she could let go and know that Hashem is above all the houses. All she needs to focus on is doing the best she can in her situation.

People are responsible for their own lives. We can help them in the way that is right for us, but we cannot live anyone else's life for them. It is our job to live our own life. We can care about others, however, this must be done from our house — from a strong place within ourselves, not out of fear or guilt. We can ask ourselves, "Is this in my house? Is this my responsibility?" If we are not sure, we can check with someone else who can help us gain clarity about the situation. In this way, when it is the right thing for us to help another person, it comes from our house, and we can give in a powerful way that leaves us energized, not drained.

Looking for the Health Within

Sometimes we meet someone who is unfriendly or impolite. It is easy to get stuck on this behavior and begin to think, *What a grumpy person!* or *What's wrong with her?* Think of it in this way. When you go to a store and it is closed, the shutters are down. Still, there is a well-stocked store behind those shutters. When a person gives off an uncaring attitude, their "shutters" are down, but behind the shutters is the real person. Instead of getting put off by the shutters, we can trust what is behind the shutters, knowing that behind those shutters is the real person.

Dalia had a hard time getting along with her sister Hadassah. They often annoyed each other, sometimes ending up in serious fights. Hadassah would often ignore Dalia when she asked her something, and this would make her mad. Once Dalia began to understand more about people and how their "shutters" can come down when they feel unsure of themselves or insecure in some way, she stopped getting so bothered by how Hadassah acted when she was in a bad space in herself. She stopped taking Hadassah's "shutters" personally and getting stuck in them. She began to see the bigger picture of Hadassah, and although Hadassah still drove her crazy sometimes, she knew that this was not the real Hadassah and it was worth waiting for the real Hadassah to surface.

How to Speak So People Will Listen

Michal did not know what to do. She wanted to discuss dropping a subject in school with her parents, but she knew that they had very strong opinions about it. She really felt that this was the right thing for her, and she wanted to give it her best shot. She definitely wanted to try something different from the last time she'd brought up the subject, when her parents ended up yelling at her and she froze and couldn't say anything.

Michal was amazed that when she spoke confidently, respectfully, and to the point, her parents took her so much more seriously. Here are her tips:

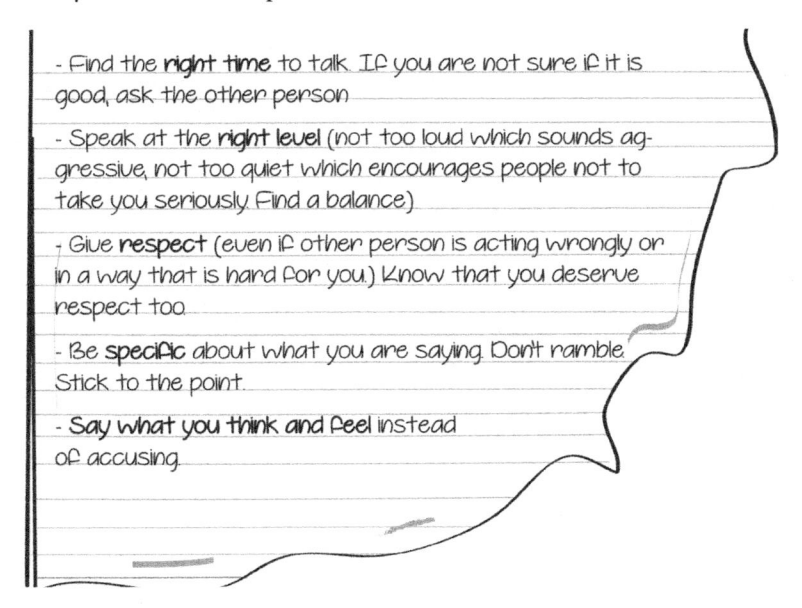

- Find the **right time** to talk. If you are not sure if it is good, ask the other person
- Speak at the **right level** (not too loud which sounds aggressive, not too quiet which encourages people not to take you seriously. Find a balance)
- Give **respect** (even if other person is acting wrongly or in a way that is hard for you.) Know that you deserve respect too.
- Be **specific** about what you are saying. Don't ramble. Stick to the point.
- **Say what you think and feel** instead of accusing.

This is not a guarantee that people will do what you want, but following these tips means that you know you are doing the best you can from your house.

What Other Teens Have Said About Secret 6

If you don't have boundaries, you feel worn out and let people take advantage of you.

Be open with your good friends.

If you are doing something right and you think someone will make fun of you, just think about what you would think deep down if you saw someone else doing the same thing.

Be yourself. Don't try to be anyone else.

SECRET 7

Stress Comes from Your Mind, Not from Life

Let me introduce you to Ruti — a very stressed-out Ruti. She feels so tense. Now, it may seem like Ruti is stressed because her teacher is annoyed with her, because she has loads of homework, or because she has a difficult situation going on at home. The truth is that she is stressed because her mind has sped up too quickly and she is getting distracted from the calm within her. Stress comes from her thinking, not from her life. Ruti's mind has started to speed up with lots of thoughts about different people and different situations in her life. What does Ruti need? Well, the first thing she needs to do is to slow down.

Homework
Diary
2x + 3by
9ab
SCHOOL
Explain th
significanc
the Battle
ENGLIS
Karen Keet

Slow-Down Signal

Have you ever noticed electric signs at the side of the road that measure your speed and flash if you're going too fast? Occasionally, I can be driving along, and when I see what my speed is, I realize that I have been going too fast without noticing. This is my signal that I need to slow down.

Stress is our "flashing sign" letting us know that we are going too fast and need to slow down. I don't mean that we have to start moving more slowly, I mean that *our mind* needs to slow down. Stress is like a flashing sign telling us that our thinking has gotten too quick, we are thinking about too many things at once, our insecurities are taking over our mind, and we need to slow down, quiet our mind, and find new direction. It is time to take our focus off the details until we regain our confidence and focus.

The Water Pipe

The water pipe in my kitchen is watertight, so when we turn on the tap, a steady, powerful flow of water comes out. I imagine our energy that we get in each moment in the same way. It is a steady, powerful flow. It contains everything we need to be okay in that moment —wisdom, clarity, trust, acceptance, and confidence. It is all coming to us. When we catch this energy, we feel energized and motivated.

Sometimes, we innocently create holes in the "pipe," and the energy starts to "leak out." This is when our mind fills with thoughts about other things and we get distracted from what is real in the moment. As soon as we do this, the energy starts to get diluted and weakened. This is when we start to feel that we can't deal with life and become hopeless and generally stressed-out. The good news is, there is a fresh, watertight pipe in every moment, so even if we were distracted in the moment before, the new moment comes and there is a new chance to make use of our powerful resources.

The Bowling Game

Dina, Tali, and Esther decide to go bowling during midwinter vacation.

Dina steps up for her turn but is distracted by everyone else's bowling alley instead of focusing on her own.

Tali starts thinking about being disappointed with her last turn and worrying about her future turns instead of focusing on now.

Esther steps up for her turn, focuses on her ball and pins right in this moment, this turn, doing the best she can and... gets a strike!

Little does Esther know that she has given us some really important pointers for how to deal with overwhelming feelings. Here are her rules:

Rule number 1: Keep your eyes on your aisle instead of being distracted by other people's aisles. (Focus on yourself instead of being pulled by others.) We have discussed this in chapter 6.

Rule number 2: Keep focused on the present moment instead of getting distracted by the past or the future. (Focus on the now.) We will discuss this in chapter 8.

Rule number 3: Keep focused on the present shot instead of getting distracted by other shots. (Focus on what you have to deal with now instead of getting distracted or overwhelmed by all you will have to do in the future.) We will discuss this in chapter 9.

What Other Teens Have Said About Secret 7

> *It's good to know that everyone feels stressed-out sometimes. We are not alone.*

> **Focusing on one thing at a time really helps me to calm down and stop getting so stressed-out!**

> Sometimes I picture the 'bowling game' and it reminds me to focus.

SECRET 8

Let Go of the Past and Stop Worrying About the Future

Rina had found her first year of high school very difficult. She had suffered from headaches, which had affected her studies. On the first day of tenth grade, she felt like she had a pit in her stomach, almost like she was carrying the whole of last year in it! She began to dread the year ahead, worrying that it would be a disaster.

The temperature in my dining room is usually comfortable. Sometimes, however, the back door and the front door are open at the same time, and as I am sitting on my couch, I can suddenly feel the discomfort of a cold breeze. If I close the doors, it will be warm again.

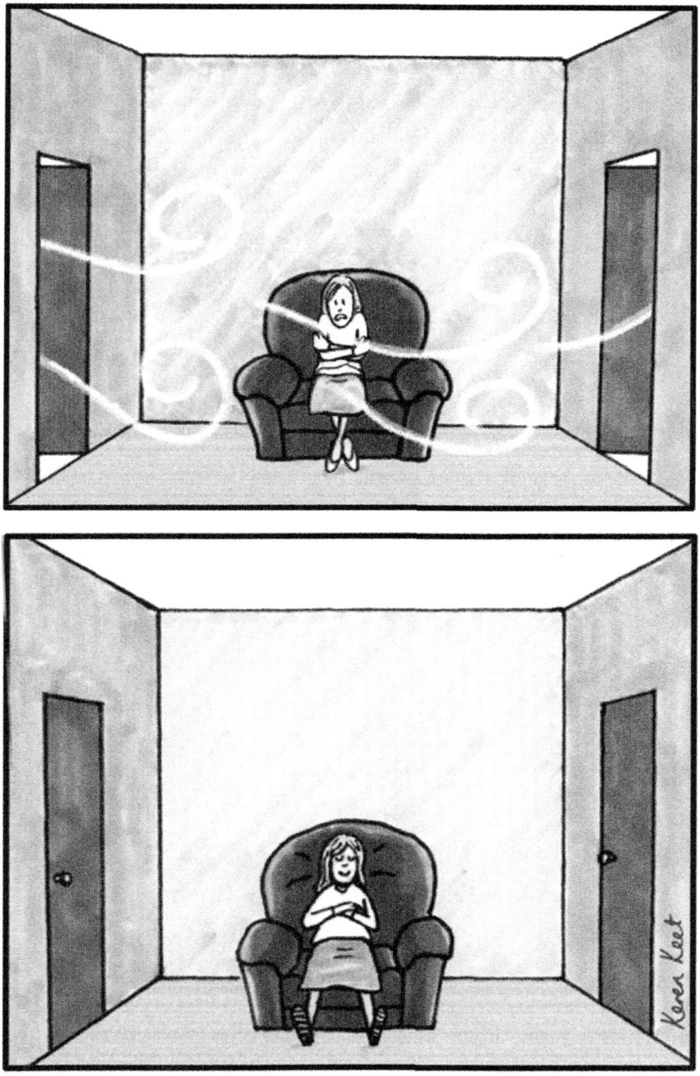
Karen Keet

Rina could "close the back door" — she could let go of her experiences in her first year of high school — and "close the front door" — stop worrying about how the future year would be. As Rina did this, she was able to focus on the moment of being right there, in her classroom on that day, and she started to feel far more focused, hopeful, and empowered.

> Do memories from the past bother you? Do you worry about the future? What would you like to 'close the door' on?

When I watch little children play, I see what it means to be in the moment. They are so focused on the Magna-Tiles or Lego that they are playing with. As they play, the whole world stands still! All that is real is right in front of them. They focus on it, they enjoy it, and they are creative in how to use it best. They are not worrying about the fact that they fell an hour ago and banged their knee or worrying about what will happen tomorrow. They are in the moment.

Each moment is an island, an independent entity completely separate from what came before it and what will come after it.

When we understand this, we can be free from getting stuck in the past or obsessing about the future. We can show up in the next moment free and open.

We Can Let Our Thinking "Grow Up"

Fifteen-year-old Michal had an intense fear of the dentist. She would get so stressed-out when she was outside the dentist's room that she would feel dizzy and nauseous. She would literally shake with fear. Michal had had a negative experience at the dentist as a five-year-old. At that point, she had collected some thinking and subconsciously put it into a bag. There were thoughts like "I can't do this," "The dentist wants to hurt me," and "I can't do dentists." Whenever she went to the dentist, without realizing it, she would take out that bag and release all the insecure thinking so that she would experience the same fear as she'd had as a five-year-old. Even though she was actually fifteen, she was experiencing the dentist *as if* she was five.

I asked Michal to draw a picture of her visit to the dentist when she was five and was amazed at the details she included. She remembered where each dental instrument was, where all the chairs were in the room, and who was sitting in each one. Michal began to understand that underneath her fearful thinking she has a flow of trusting thinking which is rooted in the truth that she is absolutely capable of going through the experience of going to the dentist.

Later, when all the thinking had cleared, she said, "The dentist is not so bad; why did I make such a fuss?" This was her fifteen-year-old thinking coming through, which matched what was actually going on in the moment.

Imagine trying to squeeze into an outfit you wore when you were five. It would be too small and totally outdated! Sometimes, even many years after we go through scary or upsetting experiences, we feel that we have to continue to live out that thinking. The good news is that we can update our wardrobe! We are not the same person we were then. This is a new moment. (Sometimes we need help to restock our wardrobe with new, gorgeous clothes — we need help to understand and heal from past experiences; if you need this, it is a confident move to reach out for it.)

Miri was constantly worrying about the future: *What if I have a fight with my friend? What if I get loads of homework? What if something bad happens?* She found that often, these thoughts came when she was enjoying herself. They would creep up, tap her on the shoulder, and distract her from enjoying her friends or doing the work that she was in the middle of.

Miri began to realize that Hashem is in control of the future and that it is out of her hands. She can give herself permission to let go of it. Worrying just destroys her enjoyment and appreciation of her life.

When we can relax with this knowledge, we can let ourselves focus with the understanding that all else is in Hashem's hands. We can stop trying to control things that we can't, and our stress disappears.

The Best ATM Machine

One day, I was walking with some of my children, and we passed a homeless person sitting at the side of the street. I explained that some people are so poor that they do not have any money to pay for a place to live in. One of my kids looked very concerned and asked, "Why don't they just go to the ATM machine?" Of course, we know the answer to that! There is no point in going to an ATM machine if there is nothing in the account to withdraw.

You may be interested to know about an 'account' that was set up in your name when you were born. When each of us was born, we received a "debit card" for an account with unlimited funds deposited by Hashem. At any time, we can go to the ATM machine and make a withdrawal from our account by asking for help. Hashem wants to give to us, but sometimes we need to choose what type of withdrawal we want to make.

We never need to be "homeless"; we can always use the "ATM machine." What do we need? You know how when you withdraw money, some suggested amounts come on the screen for you to select from? You can also put in another amount if you choose to. Here are some suggestions of what you may want to withdraw from your "ATM machine" when you are feeling challenged:

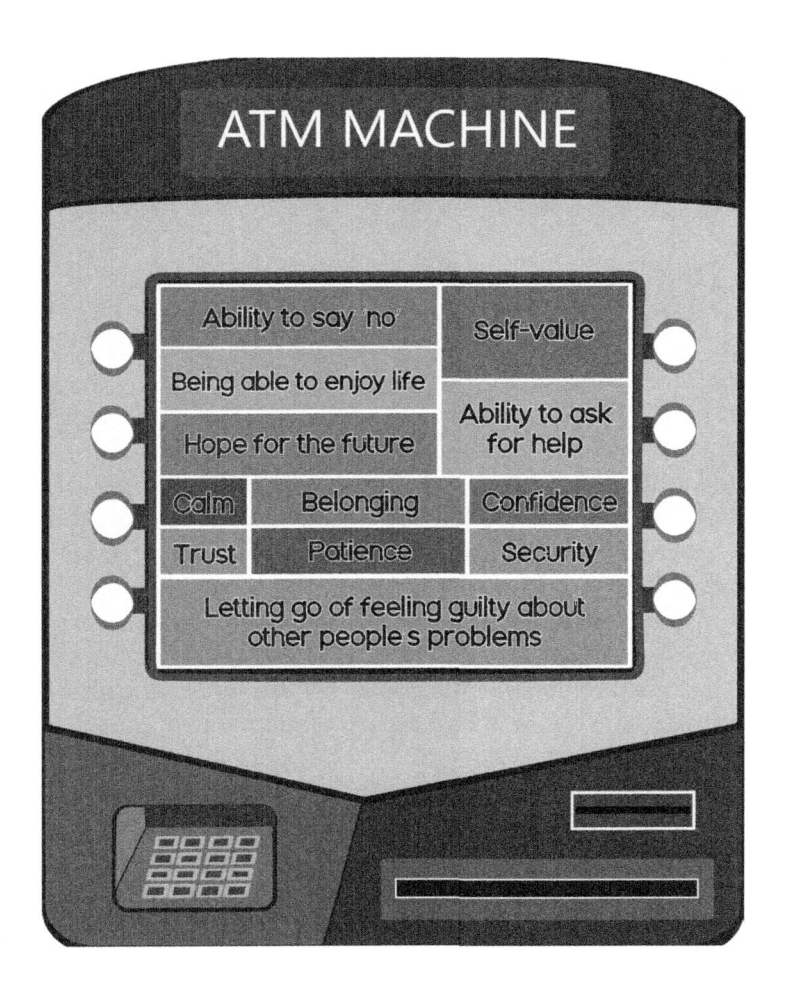

ATM MACHINE

- Ability to say 'no'
- Self-value
- Being able to enjoy life
- Hope for the future
- Ability to ask for help
- Calm
- Belonging
- Confidence
- Trust
- Patience
- Security
- Letting go of feeling guilty about other people's problems

Let me give you an example. Tamara dreaded her grandparents coming to stay at her house. As much as she liked her grandparents, they always seemed to be arguing with her parents. She didn't like seeing people she cares about hurting each other.

Tamara decided that she needed to "cash in" on some resources to help her for her grandparents' upcoming visit. She pictured her grandparents and parents arguing with each other. She then asked herself, "What would I want to withdraw from the ATM machine to help me in this situation? What strengths do I need to help me feel better?" Then she wrote a list. Here it is:

- The ability to let go of responsibility for other people's problems
- The courage to ask for help
- The ability to reach out to others
- Calm
- Hope

Tamara imagined withdrawing each of these strengths and breathing them in so that they were safely inside her. She then pictured a big argument going on again. She imagined how she would feel about it and deal with it with all these resources inside her. She felt way more relaxed when she understood that this is not her problem and she doesn't need to carry the argument on her shoulders.

Tamara's grandparents arrived, and she practiced this exercise regularly to help her cope. Once, as she was doing this exercise, she glanced out of her window and noticed her friend Sonia passing by. She went out and started talking to her. Though she wasn't comfortable enough to tell Sonia what was going on, she mentioned that it was stressful at home and she could use a good brisk walk. So, off they went! When she came back, she could see that her mother was upset and offered to make her a tea, which she knew she would appreciate. It was worth the smile it put on her face!

Tamara couldn't believe how differently she felt about the whole situation when she was able to draw on the right resources.

Think of a situation that you struggle with. What would you take out of the "ATM machine"? How would it improve the situation? Picture yourself in that situation with all these strengths inside you. How would you think, feel, or act?

What Other Teens Have Said About Secret 8

> It's good to know that we can 'cash in' on resources.

> When I start worrying about the future, I imagine myself 'closing the front door.' It helps the stress.

> I sometimes think about past memories that make me sad. It's good to know that I don't need to be stuck there.

SECRET 9

You Can Deal with Life One Moment at a Time

Stop Juggling

My son is a skilled juggler. He can juggle balls, rings, and even fire clubs. He enjoys juggling, and it's fun to watch him. Imagine, however, if he would begin to juggle throughout the day. That would mean as he is eating breakfast in the morning, as he is traveling to school, as he is sitting through his lessons, and as he is chatting with his friends or playing football during recess, he is juggling. How enjoyable would his juggling be then? How interfering would he begin to find it?

Sometimes we do the same thing in our own mind. We juggle all the different things we need to do, and it can get rather distracting!

We do not need to get our mind around everything we have to do at once. We can let ourselves focus on the right activity in each moment, knowing and trusting that we will deal with things as we need to.

One Step at a Time

Fifteen-year-old Miri and thirteen-year-old Yael were traveling together from England to Eretz Yisrael via Brussels, Belgium. As they were on their way to Manchester Airport, they started to worry about catching their connecting flight in Brussels since they only had a one-hour stopover there.

Miri and Yael had two different ways in which they could go through their journey to Eretz Yisrael. One was to focus on each stage as it came and do the best they could at each point. The second was to try to deal with the whole journey at once and feel stressed and out of control. Which do you think would be the more enjoyable way?

If you knew that you only need to deal with one thing at a time, how would you feel?

Handing the Marbles Back

Once, when one of my daughters was younger, she was overtired and in a bad mood. I had bought her some marbles to play with, and she had been having a great time with them, but now she was trying to hold eight marbles at once and was getting very frustrated because they kept dropping on the floor. I said to her, "Give your marbles to me, and I will hold them for you. You go get a cup from the kitchen to put them into." She went to get a cup, we put the marbles in, and she calmed down.

When life starts to feel heavy, overwhelming, or stressful, this is our sign that our mind is getting flooded with thoughts about many different situations. We are struggling to hold so much, and we are feeling the result. Hashem is offering us to drop the "marbles" into His strong, steady, capable hands, and we can just focus on the next action we need to take. This helps us to ease back into the present and catch the powerful energy we are being given in the moment. Hashem offers to hold all aspects of life for us — our friendships, our studies, our health, our home life, our personal growth . . . He will hold them for us if we let go of them and give them to Him, and we can then be freed up to focus on the necessary activity of the moment.

Put Down Your Heavy Bags

Hashem is "driving" us through life. He is the One Who is giving us the ideas, the strength, and the ability to deal with any situation that comes up. We can relax and "put down" our stresses. No matter what we are dealing with, we can either pretend that we can manage on our own or admit to the reality that Hashem is carrying us through life anyway, so we might as well enjoy the ride!

When we realize that we are being carried, our stress can really go down. We do not need to get our mind around everything. Hashem is carrying it all for us. We just need to take responsible action; we need to do the best we can in any given situation.

The Forest Bear

A man is walking in a forest and comes across a huge, angry bear. In his panic, he grabs a branch, aims it like a rifle, and shoots.

The bear drops dead! The man sees himself as a miracle worker...

Until he realizes where the shot actually came from...

Clara is very artistic. She used to get very nervous before she needed to complete any art assignment. She would overthink her ideas and get very stressed and uptight. Once she began to realize that although she was the one making the drawings, it was really Hashem Who was sending them to her, she began to relax. The shot was not coming from her, she just had to go through the motions of drawing, of doing her best, and the result would come from Above. Interestingly, as she relaxed, her creative talent came through much more easily and she got some great drawings done.

Avital used to get very intense about things. She would obsess about a problem until she found a solution. She felt that she had to constantly think about things until they were sorted out, whether it was a problem at school or at home. As she began to realize that sometimes things take time to settle and some solutions come in stages, she experienced a major shift in her thinking. She began to see that she cannot hurry up the process. It will take the time it needs to take, and she can either be stressed-out and impatient or do what she can at each stage and then sit back and enjoy watching the process unfold. She began to see that the solution does not come from her mind, it comes from Hashem, and therefore she can rest her mind from thinking about it all the time and trust that if she keeps taking responsible action, Hashem will send the solution in the time that He knows is perfect. It's like a child who is on a journey and asks "Are we there yet?" every five minutes. He doesn't understand that the journey takes five hours, and he can either rest and enjoy it or be impatient.

Now, when there is a difficult situation going on for Avital, she focuses on it, does whatever she has to, and then enjoys chatting with a friend, relaxing with a book, or just engaging in life. She used to think that not thinking about a situation meant that she did not care about it and that it would slow down her ability to reach an answer. She now sees that the solution comes from a far deeper and more profound source than her mind, and even though, of course, she needs to work things through at the right time, she does not need to be tense and uptight about it. She can trust that Hashem will unfold things at the right time in the right way.

I experienced exactly the same process when I wrote this book. There were a lot of different aspects, details, and people involved. I could either get overwhelmed and stressed or focus in each moment on what I needed to then. Each moment had its own job description, and that is what I was in control of; how the whole thing came together was out of my control. Letting go was great! I could just take one step at a time. I am happy with the result. I hope you are too!

> If you knew that Hashem runs the world and you just need to do your bit what would this change?

What Other Teens Have Said About Secret 9

> It feels so much better to take things one step at a time. I like knowing that it's my job to do my best and that I can let go of the rest.

> I like to remember that Hashem is carrying me. I feel safe and cared about.

BRINGING IT ALL TOGETHER

WATCH: Four Steps to Your Teen Power

It happens to the best of us! We get caught up in insecure thinking/feeling, which can have a very strong pull to it. Here are some tips to help us navigate it, based on the secrets we have discovered.

WWhat are you feeling? This may seem obvious, but how often do we not even realize that we are feeling insecure in some way? Before we know it, we may be arguing with someone or feeling like the world is a sad place! Realizing what we are feeling is a very important step in dealing with anything. Ask yourself, "What am I feeling? What simulator am I in? What's up with me?"

AAccept: Don't panic about what you are feeling. Allow yourself to feel without feeling silly, weak, or the need to force the feeling out. It is okay. It's okay to be wherever you are right now. Let yourself be there. You — the whole, healthy you — have stepped into a simulator. You are still valuable, no matter what. You can get off your wobble board!

TTrust: Even as you are in the simulator, there is a calm room surrounding the simulator. Hashem is holding everything. Let go of what you cannot control. Trust yourself to deal with what you can.

CHCHoose: Don't just react automatically to how you feel. Within what you are experiencing — within what you know to be true — what is the best way to act now? No matter what is happening outside of your "house," you have the potential to choose well. Is there any action to take that could help you feel better, such as taking a walk, listening to music, or speaking to someone who could help the situation? Is there anything you feel is right to do to help anyone else who is relevant? If you knew that you have the power inside you to choose well, what would you do now? What do you actually have to deal with now, in this moment?

Here is an example of someone who put the above stages into action:

Yocheved, aged fourteen, had been counting down to her two-week vacation with her cousins in Italy. She had spent hours deciding what she was going to do each day and had saved up her allowance for months to pay for all the exciting outings on her itinerary. But the day before she was supposed to travel, she tripped and broke her leg in two places, necessitating surgery to reset the bone. She could not believe it! She would not be able to go!

Yocheved worked through the WATCH stages. See for yourself:

What am I feeling?
I am feeling disappointed and annoyed. I'm all over the place! I can't believe what has happened! Honestly, I can't imagine ever being okay about this.

Accept
It is okay that I feel like this, it's not silly or weak. Phew! That's a relief; this is a big challenge for me. I'm not scared of my feelings.

Trust
I can let go of the whole situation. It is in Hashem's hands. I can't control it. It's not my fault that I fell; it was supposed to happen. I trust myself to deal with the situation well. I have what it takes.

Choose
I couldn't control what happened but I can control the way I respond to it. And I am going to! I can either feel sorry for myself and get stuck in this, or I can try to help myself. Hey, that feels better! I think tomorrow I'll discuss with my parents if we can rebook the trip for a different time so that I'll have it to look forward to.

Yocheved definitely felt stronger after going through the four stages. Good for her!

FINAL WORDS

I hope you enjoyed reading this book as much as I enjoyed writing it for you. My advice to you is to keep reading it. Each time you read it, you will probably gain something new, depending on the mood you are in or situations you are involved with. My hope is that you find confidence and success in your life and, most of all, that you realize what an exquisite person you are and live your life in a way that reflects that.

With warmest wishes,
Deborah Saunders

APPROBATIONS

Torah Umesorah Publications

Rabbi Shmuel Yaakov Klein, Director

ב"ה

August, 2020
Menachem Av, 5780

To whom it may concern:

I have had the pleasure of perusing – and reading a number of portions of – Mrs. D. Saunders' soon-to-be released work, *Teen Power – for Girls*. This important book will foreseeably make a significant impact on the way that young people navigate through the numerous social-emotional challenges that arise in their lives.

The primary approach is to help reduce the anxiety that is so often associated with the various scenarios. This is done through the use of a friendly and conversational style for the sharing of ideas... as well as by making use of day-to-day analogies that are familiar and easy to comprehend. Mrs. Saunders thus gives meaningful perspectives into everyday issues and offers coping strategies to help the young reader (or the older one for that matter!).

Of very special importance, however, is the additional feature that *Teen Power* puts a crucial Yiddishkeit spin on the topics at hand, providing valuable *chizuk* in areas of *emunah* and *bitachon*.

Teen Power should become either required reading or a handy resource for consultation for today's young student, who lives in a world that becomes increasingly complicated in the area of interpersonal relationships.

I wish Mrs. Saunders much *hatzlachah* in this as well as in future endeavors.

Rabbi Shmuel Yaakov Klein

APPROBATIONS

Rabbi Shimon Russell. L.C.S.W.

Rimon 6/8 רימון
Jerusalem ירושלים
Israel ישראל
Tel: 972 (0)587320161

26/10/20

To whom it may concern:

It is my pleasure to recommend "Teen Power - 9 secrets to confidence & success" by Mrs. D. Saunders.

Mrs. Saunders has written a much needed book to help our regular mainstream teenage girls. She presents the challenges of *today's* teenagers, & skilfully provides insight & practical down to earth resources to help them navigate their journey through their often turbulent teenage years. This is a must read for all teenage girls seeking to strive for excellence, while remaining healthy, balanced & grounded.

Rabbi Shimon Russell

APPROBATIONS

RABBI DOVID GOLDWASSER
KHAL BAIS YITZCHOK

הרב דוד גאלדוואסער
מרא דאתרא ד'קהל בית יצחק,
ברוקלין ניו יארק

חמשה עשר באב, תש"פ

I write this letter on behalf of Deborah Saunders, a dedicated worker on behalf of Klal Yisroel, who has published yet another important volume on emotional health and wellbeing. Infused with the Torah perspective and *hashkafically* inspirational citations, the book is an invaluable tool to help the reader face the demands and challenges of life with faith, awareness, and hope.

From her work as a counselor and psychotherapist, she has collected many interesting case histories and stories with advice and guidance on critical issues of today's generation. The book, *Teen Power*, contains a wealth of knowledge as to how teens in particular can gain self-confidence and self-empowerment. She provides clear-cut examples, diagrams that greatly help to clarify salient points in self-development. Some of the issues addressed are insecurity, self-confidence, anxiety, moods and emotions, self-acceptance, self-esteem, and dealing with criticism.

The great Belzer Rebbe זצוק"ל makes an interesting comment on the *pasuk* in *Tehillim* (90:10) – ימי שנותינו בהם שבעים שנה" – the days of our years among them are seventy years ..." He notes that each of the seven teen age years has the power to impact ten years of one's adult life. How fitting it is that the author chose *Teen Power*, as the title of her book, particularly because of the unique power that is deeply-rooted within each and every *bas Yisroel*.

It is my every hope and prayer that this book will take its well-earned place, next to the author's earlier book, *Being and Becoming*, in the libraries of professionals and laymen alike throughout the world. I wish the author much *hatzlacha* in this endeavor and in all her efforts on behalf of the *klal*. May she be *zoche* to be counted among the מצדיקי הרבים שצדקתם עומדת לעד.

המצפה לישועות ה'

Rabbi Dovid Goldwasser

2016 AVENUE I · BROOKLYN, NY 11210 · TEL. 718-339-4582 / STUDY 718-677-3712

APPROBATIONS

FEDERATION BEIS DIN · בית דין

65 Watford Way, London NW4 3AQ
T 020 8202 2263　F 020 8203 0610
beisdin@federation.org.uk
federation.org.uk

בס"ד

הרב שרגא פייבל הלוי זיממערמאן
רב ואב"ד

To whom it may concern:

I looked through the material written by Mrs D Saunders which will be published as "Teen Power for Girls" — I believe it is a valuable addition to the body of material written about chinuch — It specifically addresses the challenges of teen girls in our era — It gives them tools to deal with current issues from both an emotional perspective & a spiritual one

APPROBATIONS

Rabbi Zev Leff

Rabbi of Moshav Matityahu
Rosh HaYeshiva—Yeshiva Gedola Matityahu

בס"ד

הרב זאב לף

מרא דאתרא מושב מתתיהו
ראש הישיבה—ישיבה גזולה מתתיהו

| D.N. Modiin 71917 | Tel: 08-976-1138 טל' | Fax: 08-976-5326 פקס' | ד.נ. מודיעין 71917 |

Dear Friends,

I have read portions of "Teen Power for Girls" by Deborah Saunders.

Teenagers are going through serious physical and emotional changes which present specific challenges. The authoress offers solid advice on aquiring positive and secure thinking, control of one's moods and emotions, self esteem, free choice and other important life skills. She also addresses emunah and bitachon in Hashem as a very important anchor to one's spiritual and emotional well being.

Although I am not a teenage girl, I found the material interesting, informative and inspiring. The material is presented in a practical down to earth manner with illustrations that help to convey and enhance the message that is presented in the text. I found the ideas presented in consanance with Torah hashkafah.

I recommend this book to teenage girls of all backgrounds and also to their parents and teachers who are grappling with guiding their daughters and students to successfully navigate this difficult but most important stage in their lives.

I commend the authoress on a quality presentation and pray that Hashem bless her and her family with life, health and the wherewithal to continue to merit the community, especially with a sequel for teenage boys.

Sincerely,
With Torah blessings

Zv Leff

Rabbi Zev Leff

APPROBATIONS

RETORNO
Addiction prevention and treatment

BH

Elul 5780

One might think an addiction prevention program would offer slogans warning of the dangers of experimentation. In fact, Retorno's addiction prevention programs focus primarily on emotions – identifying, accepting, and sharing emotions. The reason for this is because addiction, codependency, and other maladaptive behaviors stem from a need to escape fear, sadness, and other painful feelings and thoughts. If one can learn to accept and deal with emotion, s/he will do so without turning to dangerous alternative means of escape.

Unfortunately, many people confront their emotional world only *after* they have entered into a committed relationship (i.e. marriage), and begin to experience difficulties.

This book is an important resource that puts teenagers in touch with their emotional world. Without placing a heavy burden of introspection on the reader, it normalizes common beliefs, offers insights, and promotes emotional education.

Shoshana Schwartz
International Liaison, Retorno
Addiction & Codependency Counselor
EFT Practitioner
Therapeutic Riding Instructor

APPROBATIONS

Deborah Saunders masterfully uses examples and stories of everyday-life to provide truths and perspectives that can empower us to live our lives with calm and confidence.

Rabbi Yoel Gold

APPROBATIONS

Deborah Saunders is brilliant at using metaphor to help us concretize and overcome challenges. This book will be invaluable in calming the emotional turbulence teens experience and empowering them to come out on top.

Gila Manolson

Printed in Great Britain
by Amazon